KICK EM
- IN THE -
GUTS
COWBOY TO CAV.

FRANK O STEPHENS

Kick Em In The Guts
Copyright © 2019 by Frank O Stephens

All rights reserved. No part of this publication may be reproduced, distributed, or transmitted in any form or by any means, including photocopying, recording, or other electronic or mechanical methods, without the prior written permission of the author, except in the case of brief quotations embodied in critical reviews and certain other non-commercial uses permitted by copyright law.

Tellwell Talent
www.tellwell.ca

ISBN
978-0-2288-1671-3 (Hardcover)
978-0-2288-1670-6 (Paperback)
978-0-2288-1672-0 (eBook)

ABOUT THE AUTHOR

AUTHOR AND RAT ROD

Mr. Stephens lives in Nevada, where a man can ride a horse and wear a six-shooter to coffee at the local Starbucks, if you can stand the bad coffee. He has recently gotten his first rat rod and looks forward to feeling the wind where his hair used to be.

He tries to always have a good sense of humor; the world can be a tough place but it is ridiculous at the same time. Life is too short not to enjoy it.

Mr. Stephens is now living and experiencing life for the vets who never came home. He would like you to join him in lifting a glass, a joint, or a bong hit to all the warriors—past and present—who served their country.

INTRODUCTION

There are very few first-person accounts of armored cavalry units in the Vietnam War. I do not tell my story as an expert in the field. Far from it. I retired after my first tour and have not regretted it.

We were able to go almost anywhere we wanted and the scenery was, and still is, stunning. I guess you could say I saw Vietnam before the world really changed it. My life and Vietnam have been entangled for over fifty years, both as a feared enemy and an ardent lover. I learned so much from her and she is still teaching me.

I know that music is important to my memories of a time and place. My memories of Vietnam begin with "Louie, Louie" by the Kingsmen, and continue with Eric Burdon's "We Gotta Get Out of This Place," "House of the Rising Sun," and "Sky Pilot." When my track mates heard I was a Mormon and was a priesthood holder, they asked me if I was some kinda sky pilot. So, I had a nickname.

My Black track mates had a little pink .45 record player that never ran out of batteries and I heard "I Heard it Through the Grapevine" 45 billion times. When it became the raisin song, I had flashbacks to the war.

And let's not forget Credence Clearwater Revival's "Fortunate Son," "Proud Mary," and "Run Through the

Jungle." I was sent a copy of The Moody Blues' "Nights in White Satin." Those songs take me back.

This book is my first-person account of what it was like for a 19-year-old to experience combat. In the writing of this book, I have learned a lot about what actually happened, not just what I remember. My mind has hidden a lot of ugly and shocking memories from me.

In my research for this book I learned that my unit had been engaged in far more contact than I remembered, in my 11 months and 13 days in the country.

I mostly remember the heat and dirt and being bone-tired all the time, and still pulling two hours of guard at night, but I learned so much, so fast that I lost all my childhood illusions in a hurry.

I saw firsthand how cruel man can be to fellow man. When in combat, there are no higher moral standards to abide by, just the survival instinct. Ideals are no good to dead men.

"Kick 'Em in the Guts"

When I was very young, I sat at the Otto Stephens Cowboy Club and Golden Spur Café in Afton, Wyoming, and listened to the old hands talk about *cowboyin'* and such. My uncle, Ed Harris, ex-OSS agent, became station chief in Singapore in the 1950s, then known as the CIA. Uncle Ed told me that when I was very young the cowboys would pay me to say, as loud as I could, "KICK 'EM IN THE GUTS!"

MIKE AND FRANK WITH HORSE

FRANK ON PONY

LITTLE COWBOY

I have used this as a call to press ahead, or as the 10th Cavalry motto says, "READY AND FORWARD." I was born to be a Buffalo Soldier.

DEDICATION

This book is dedicated to all the Vietnam Veterans who served in-country and offshore who can still read a book.

It was my honor to serve with the fine men of the 10th Cavalry. When the unit was created, it was an all-Black unit except for the officers. There were more Medal of Honor winners than in any other unit, but they were not awarded until they were dead. Racism sucks.

My advice to you is go back to Vietnam as a visitor as soon as you can and as often as you can. It has helped me more with my PTSD than any group or drug ever did.

Congratulations, you are now part of a dying breed! We are a lost generation who hid in plain sight.

I have been turned down for a job because I was a Vietnam veteran and we were not to be trusted. My experiences both before and after the war have taught me a lot of things. Forgiveness is one of them. But I will never forget how this country treated us after our tours.

Now, a coward and a draft dodger is President (excuse me, Little Donnie Trump). He hates Mr. Mueller, who is a decorated Vietnam vet and hero. Also, he insulted John McCain. Do you see a common thread? They are both Vietnam vets. I am sorry that you weren't brave enough to fight, but leave us who did alone.

ACKNOWLEDGMENTS

A very special thanks to my friend and life partner, Elisa Hickey, who has helped me at every step along the way.

And thank you to Ron Miska for a lot of the information and pictures in this book. I could not have done this without your help.

TABLE OF CONTENTS

PROLOGUE "Here We Go" 1
Chapter 1   Some History 3
Chapter 2   My War Glossary 12
Chapter 3   A Week and Three Days Early 21
Chapter 4   If You Ain't Cavalry, You Ain't Shit 26
Chapter 5   Get Used to It; You Are In-Country Now! 28
Chapter 6   Now for the Real Story 33
Chapter 7   Mistakes Can Kill Ya 42
Chapter 8   The Best Damn Monkey Story 46
Chapter 9   But They Are on Our Side, Aren't They? 50
Chapter 10 There Are Traps Everywhere 58
Chapter 11 Mud in Ban Me Thuot 62
Chapter 12 Dusted Off 88
Chapter 13 My Welcome Home 101
Chapter 14 Comedy Years 108
Chapter 15 Sun Dance Years 111
Chapter 16 Family History 116
Chapter 17 Return to Ambush Site 126

PROLOGUE
"Here We Go"

As I stepped off the plane on April 15, 1968, in Cam Ranh Bay, Vietnam, the air met me like an ill-fitting suit, a suit I would wear uncomfortably for the next 11 months and 13 days in combat. I found my way there, with the army's help, and it couldn't have been any more alien from the Rocky Mountain high of Star Valley, Wyoming, which still looks much the same as it did when I was born on December 29, 1948. As I was soon to find out, once Vietnam runs her exotic fingers over your soul, you are never the same.

CHAPTER 1
Some History

My name is Frank Otto Stephens. I was born December 29, 1948, in Afton, Wyoming. My father was Vaughn Thomas Stephens and my mother was Mrs. Rhea Iverson (Jaques). She passed away October 23, 2017. She was 94 years old and I am a mommy's boy. I owe these two people everything I am and ever will be. I'm thankful for good genes; they are a gift from the past.

Both my father and I are combat veterans. My father served in the Pacific Theater in an artillery outfit and was in the invasion of Leyte Gulf, Philippines, October 23–26, 1944.

VAUGHN STEPHENS IN CLASS-A UNIFORM

FRANK STEPHENS IN CLASS-A UNIFORM

Frank O Stephens

I served in Vietnam on a mortar track assigned to the 10th Armored Cavalry from April 15, 1968, till I was wounded on March 2, 1969.

I was drafted from the state of Utah, November 15, 1967. I reported to the draft center in downtown Salt Lake City, Utah.

After a long induction and physical examination process, we were loaded on a bus and driven to the airport and flown to Fort Lewis, Washington, via Travis Air Force Base.

We arrived late in the afternoon and were subjected to the standard harassment and abuse from the drill sergeants. We ran from place to place, and, of course, it started to rain sometime around 1:00 a.m. We were marched to a parking lot and told that if we wanted to re-up or become an R.A. (Regular Army) we would be allowed to go inside, out of the rain, and have coffee and a cookie. What a good trade for an extra year of your life. I did not go inside.

About 3:00 a.m., we got to bed and I started my short military life as a draftee in an army full of gung-ho types.

I was neither a hippie nor a warmonger, just a western lad trying to measure up to my father's example in WWII.

As a boy, I had gotten into my mother's cedar chest and there were my father's war ribbons. All those awards for deeds done in the war.

I wanted my own ribbons and awards and now I have them, including a Purple Heart.

I had no idea how much it would cost to gain those ribbons.

BASIC TRAINING GRADUATION

I spent my six weeks in Fort Lewis and learned many useful and some useless things. We walked and ran a lot in the rain of that winter of 1967.

At this point, I had never seen or used any illegal drugs, just beer and a little hard liquor. I bought my first cigars and Zippo lighter and got burned by the lighter fluid—a common experience for newbie smokers.

I had always been a good shot and was comfortable with firearms. I trained with an M1 Garand. Learned to fire it and clean and repair the firearm. Then, they gave us an M14 and I qualified as an expert. Two weeks before I was sent to Vietnam, they gave us a plastic thing they called an M16.

How was I supposed to use this in hand-to-hand combat? It would break in two while they laughed at you. I qualified as an expert with every weapon except the .45 caliber, 1911 pistol. I might as well just throw it at someone because I couldn't shoot them with it.

I was sent to Fort Knox, Kentucky, to be trained as an 11D-20 Scout Observer Armor Intelligence Specialist. This consisted of riding around on 113 A-1 armored personnel carriers, learning how to fire an M60, .30 caliber, belt-fed, shoulder-fired, gas-operated fully automatic weapon. There is nothing like the power of a fully automatic weapon fired by a young man; it is very intoxicating and empowering. I was the squad leader and all of my men were National Guard members from Kentucky and Tennessee. They never went to Vietnam with me.

As with most men who were drafted into the Vietnam War, I arrived alone and unassigned to any unit, knowing no one and no one knew me. There was no unit identity. I was allowed to stay in Fort Knox for two weeks to go through intensive Vietnam training. We learned to jump off of an unmoving truck, while drill instructors fired blanks over our heads. Then six-foot-tall Black men in black pajamas pretended to be VC and set booby traps that were easy to find and looked nothing like the real thing. They are now called IEDs. The Vietnamese were very good at that before it became fashionable.

FORT KNOX

FRANK IN ROOM

I was given two weeks' leave and returned to Salt Lake City, Utah. My real hometown is Henefer, Utah. It is located about 50 miles over the Wasatch Mountains in a valley settled by my family in 1847, when the Mormons settled that part of the West.

I was related to every family in the valley because of Mormon polygamy and interbreeding. My great-grandfather had three wives and thirty children. Each wife had her own house and family; they were kept separate for his peace of mind.

I had graduated from North Summit High School in June of 1967. I spent that summer in the forests of Wyoming in the Teton wilderness, packing insecticide in jerry cans on horseback. It was an eventful summer. I was in a suburban truck that rolled off of the Teton Pass. We rolled end over end eight times but no one was seriously injured.

I went into the army, November 15, 1967. I went to the draft board, which was housed in the state liquor store and talked to Mrs. Mabel Larsen. I could have gone on a mission for the Mormon Church, but I felt that I owed my country two years' service for the freedoms we enjoy. I told her that I wanted to enlist, and she suggested that if I allowed her to draft me, I would only be gone for two years instead of the typical three when you enlist. Our county was so small at that time that they only took one draftee per month, and she said that no way would she draft someone who did not want to go, so I was Summit County's choice for November 15, 1967. Thanks, Mabel.

When asked about my experienced in Vietnam and combat I usually tell them. I would not take a million dollars to do it again but, I would not take a million dollars for the lessons that it taught me about life, lessons hard earned Tell the ones you LOVE, that you Love them now today, those things that you want to do, do them NOW because you are not guaranteed one more moment, on this earth.

When I returned to Utah, I wrecked the family car, and my girlfriend, who I thought I would marry, broke up with me because she didn't know if she could be with someone who could kill another human being, she later married an Air Force bomber pilot.

I decided that I didn't want to be there any more so I reported to Fort Lewis to the unit in charge of processing the men for Vietnam. A week early.

CHAPTER 2
My War Glossary

The Vietnam War has its own words and phrases, some of which I've included here.

10th Cavalry: In the Old West, the 9th and 10th Cavalry were all-Black units. The Indians named them "Buffalo Soldiers" because their hair looked like buffalo. They were awarded their medals long after they were dead (no racism there).

AVLB: Mobile bridge for tanks and heavy trucks.

Agent Orange: Dioxin used as a defoliant over much of the country and later discovered to cause deformities in children and animals. Dow Chemical paid a settlement to the damaged in the amounted of $600.00 per person. That is not enough to pay for the damage done to children lives.

Airmobile cavalry: Fancy name for mobile infantry.

Ambush: Lying in wait to kill the enemy.

Arc Light: B-52 strikes.

ARVN: South Vietnamese Armed Forces.

BMFIC: Big Mother Fucker in Charge (i.e. the boss).

Base camp commandos: The newest statistics say that there were seven people in the rear with the gear for every field solider; they sent us the supplies.

Booby traps: Also known as IEDs.

Boonie rat: Someone who has spent a lot of time in the jungle.

Bringing pee: Putting out enough firepower to make the enemy pee their pants.

Buddhism: A religion I knew nothing about. As a group, we small-town draftees were not the most informed group. I knew Mormons and Christians, and that was it. The Buddhist religion seemed strange and exotic, much more colorful than ours.

Buffalo Soldier: See above.

Burning shit: 55-Gallon oil drums were cut in half, handles were welded on them, and then they were put under the toilet seats in the head with diesel fuel in them. We dragged them out with a long hook and sat around as the shit burned. That is a smell you never forget.

Chieu Hoi pass: Safe conduct pass, with instructions on the back.

China white: Heroin. Very pure and very, very addictive. Just after I left Vietnam in March 1969, there was beginning to be a lot of very cheap smack around. The NVA knew that if they sold us heroin, then we would take that form of slow death with us to the USA. And they were right.

Claymore anti-personnel mine: Mine with hundreds of small steel ball bearings in explosive to make a wide arc of death.

Cobra gunship: Helicopter gunship.

Concertina wire: A 50-ft. roll of barbed wire spread every night around the perimeter.

Dapping: Long, drawn-out handshakes done by the Brothers (Black men) where they rhythmically touch fists, elbows, backs of the hands and other assorted body parts. Since I am white and have no native rhythm at all, I would just watch in amazement.

DiDi Mau: Get out of here.

Door gunner: Firing an M60 machine gun out the door of a helicopter.

Deuce and a Half: Ton-and-a-half truck.

Dust-off: Some of the bravest pilots and crews that ever flew in combat. I was only on one, but that was exciting enough. Thanks again to all pilots and air crews!

F-4 Phantom jets: "Thuds," for short. They flew low and slow for a jet, and carried a lot of ordinance to drop on the other guys. I loved to see them coming in over the trees about to change someone's life. Thanks to all the pilots.

FNG: Fucking New Guy.

Fragging: Practice of rolling a hand grenade under an officer's bunk while they slept. More common than most people know.

Free-fire zone: Permission to shoot anything or anyone in a map grid area.

Fuck-you lizards: Tegu lizard whose croak sounded just like someone saying "Fuck you" in the jungle trees. I thought they must really hate us to train their lizards to swear at us in the night.

Green Berets: The Special Forces that President Kennedy created to fight a guerilla style war. I never liked the hats.

Grunts: Infantry units.

Ho Chi Minh: "Uncle Ho"—his name was everywhere. Leader of the North Vietnamese. Died in September 1969 and the Vietnamese kept it secret for a while.

Ho Chi Minh Trail: From North to South Vietnam, including parts of Laos and Cambodia, heavily bombed during the war.

CHIEU HOI PASS-FRONT

CHIEU HOI PASS-BACK

In-country R&R: If you captured a weapon or any important prisoner, you could go to Na Trang.

Indian Country: Outside the wire.

Jolly Green Giants: The Air Force rescue units based in Thailand that flew into North Vietnam to rescue downed pilots. My friend, Sergeant Joe Coburn, was a proud member of this unit. Maybe someday he will tell me about the adventures he had on three tours.

Keep your shit wired tight: A grunt term for securing your gear so it doesn't rattle in the bush.

Kill cards: Packs of cards with your unit patch on them to leave on the bodies of the enemy, so they knew who killed them.

Klick: One thousand meters.

LAW.: Light Anti-Tank Weapon made of fiberglass.

LBJ: Long Binh Jail, where they sent you for disobeying orders.

LOCH: Light Observation Helicopter. They look like little dragonflies—very fast and nimble.

Listening post: Two men with a PRC-25 radio, posted outside the wire on a trail to let the command know if anything was coming their way.

LRP: Long Range Patrol. Two-to-three–man teams behind enemy lines.

M16: New plastic 2.23 caliber, shoulder-fired, gas-operated semi-automatic personal weapon. It is designed to kill and maim anyone it hits. It is essentially a .22 with a .30 caliber punch. It exits the barrel at 3400 ft. per second. I saw a Viet Cong get hit in the hand; the hit picked him up and spun him around and exited out the side of his neck.

M79: "Blooper" 20mm grenade launcher with many different rounds, including high-explosive, shotgun, and flares.

MACV: Military Assistance Command Vietnam. US government arm of the military to train and equip the South Vietnamese.

Ma Deuce: .50 caliber machine gun

Mad Minute: A time, usually just before dark, when our whole platoon would clear our fields of fire by firing whole boxes of ammunition into the jungle in front of our positions to make sure no one was setting up any attacks.

Mama-san: Older ladies who could get you anything from a cold Coke to a hooker.

Minigun: Six-barrel machine gun firing 3000 rounds per second.

NVA: North Vietnamese Army.

Napalm: Jellied gasoline mixed with detergent to make it stick and burn at the same time.

Night vision scope: A.K.A. "starlight scope." Fuzzy green light show with little or no resolution. An early model.

No sweat: Not a problem.

Piss tube: An artillery tube, round casing or a pipe sunk into the ground at a 45-degree angle, painted OD green and filled with sand. Its use is self-explanatory.

Pot: "Grass," "smoke," or "ganja." At the time I was there, cannabis was everywhere and easy to obtain. You could get pre-rolled joints in cigarette wrappers, a whole case, for under $5.00 and pounds in bags for just dollars.

Punji stake: Bamboo stake coated with human and animal feces to cause infection.

Quad 50: Four .50 caliber M2 machine guns.

R&R: After about six months, you could go on R&R. I chose Hong Kong. It was fun and no one shot at me, but there were some adventures in that British bastion in the Orient. I will tell this story later in a chapter of its own.

Recon by fire: Shooting at something to see if anyone shoots back.

Recondo School: Jungle training done in-country in several locations.

Rock ape: A monkey in the Central Highlands that would throw rocks from the trees.

Ruff Puffs: Local militia, mostly Mountain Yards in the Central Highlands.

SEALs: US Navy special forces.

Same-same: Just what it says.

Sandies: Old Corsair prop planes flying out of Thailand for close air support.

Search and destroy: Patrols to look for and burn any extra supplies in area.

Shotgun hit: When smoking pot and someone takes a pipe and sticks the mouthpiece end into the chamber of the shotgun and blows as hard as they can into the bowl. The smoke shoots up the barrel of the gun into your mouth and lungs. Tastes of powder and gun oil.

Snoopy the Dragon: C-130 with three miniguns.

Steel pot: Steel helmet.

Thousand-yard stare: Symptom of PTSD.

Tiger cages: Bamboo cages used to torture prisoners.

Tiger stripes: Camouflage pattern for deep jungle.

Trip flares: Flares they could be set to trip with thin wire, strewn across the trail so we knew the enemy was coming.

Trooper: Any person who was assigned to a cavalry outfit whether armored or airmobile.

Tunnel rats: Small men who were brave enough to chase Viet Cong into their own tunnel systems with a flashlight and a .45 caliber pistol.

Two-step snake: Bamboo viper—two steps and you're DEAD.

UH-1: Bell helicopter nicknamed "Huey"—everyday troop carrier.

Un-ass my AO: Leave my area of operation, fast.

VC: Viet Cong. South Vietnamese who fought in the south.

Vietnamization of the Vietnam War: When our troops withdrew, the Vietnamese took over the fight. That didn't turn out well.

Willie Peter: White phosphorus. Burns through most anything until it runs out of air or fuel. A terrible weapon.

Yards: Mountain tribes named by the French to include all tribal groups in the Highlands.

CHAPTER 3
A Week and Three Days Early

We were processed all day. I received nine inoculations for things that I had never heard of, like malaria, and dengue fever. I finished at 3:00 a.m., thinking I had two more days to adjust to the shots.

But at 5:30 a.m., they woke us up and selected four of us as volunteers to complete a flight. I found myself stunned and very tired, amazed at where I was, a week and three days early for an unknown war.

I boarded a Tiger Airlines Boeing 707 with Asian stewardesses and lots of brand-new khaki uniforms. And many very nervous young men, trying to pretend that we were not scared.

The man in the seat in front of me had a grand mal seizure and a Green Beret with a well-trimmed goatee saved him from choking to death. It was only the first of many shocking and unexpected things to come.

"You Are In-Country Now"

We flew into Cam Ranh Bay to the replacement center. As we walked off the plane, we noticed that the unit was divided into incoming and outgoing, new and old. I tried to talk to some of the grunts on the other side of the fence but to them, we were just FNGs (Fucking New Guys), and they didn't want to talk to us because as one guy said, "You already dead, you just too dumb to know it. Now fuck off." I went to the barracks, kind of shocked. Those men were the same age as I was, 19 or 20, but they looked and acted much older and appeared haunted by what they had been through. Was I going to be like them when I finished my tour?

I received my orders to join B Troop 1st 10th Cavalry Headquarters, located in Pleiku, Central Highlands. It was called Camp Evans—soon to be Camp Enari—but the forward firebase was the Oasis, a few klicks from the Cambodian border. I was handed my orders and told to find my way to a C-130 idling and ready to take off.

This was the first time I had ever been allowed to board a plane while it had the rear ramp down without supervision. I sat down and was introduced to the strange world of a combat zone.

The uniform that the people were wearing was very exotic, indeed. It bore all kinds of camouflage in different patterns—no two seemed to be alike. These soldiers were ARVN—Armed Forces Vietnam. All of their uniforms were tailored and skin-tight. Later, we referred to them as cowboys—they looked really good but they seldom fought well.

I found my way to the unit headquarters and the first sergeant told me to find a bunk and wait for a ride out to the field where my unit was.

One night, a group of old salts took me out and got me quite drunk. They took me to the unit motor pool to show me something neat. What they showed me was a mortar track that had been hit by a B-40 rocket and exploded, and the whole thing looked like an exploded orange, grotesquely twisted from the concussion.

Then they told me that if I were on a mortar track and it hit a mine, they would pick up my body with a teaspoon. I did not know it then, but I would soon be assigned to a mortar track as if I were not scared enough. The next day B Troop came into base camp to refit for the field.

B-40 IN

B-40 OUT—DAMAGE INSIDE

I soon found myself on Mortar Track Number 29 with four other troopers. I am from Utah and there are very, very few Black people. Well, everyone on the track except for me was Black—culture by immersion. Needless to say, I was very nervous about my new digs and roommates.

The track commander was Sergeant Ben, whose last name I never knew. He was an ex-boxer from Detroit and he would not tie his boot laces because, as he said, if he stepped on a land mine, it would just blow him out of his loose boots. Luckily, I ever got to see him test his theory.

Then there was Cassell Lewis, with his walrus mustache and his golden tongue and bouncy demeanor. He was the most animated person I had ever met.

Since I had never been around Black people, they sat me down and had the "Black" talk with me.

Sgt. Ben said the rules were simple: You do not use the N-word that they use down South, and you do not call us "motherfuckers." Since I had never heard that particular word in my life. I did not know that would become a big part of my language from then on. And you DID NOT touch Sgt. Ben when he was sleeping, which I never intended to do. I did not know how important Lesson Number Three was, but on a dark night in Ban Me Thuot, I learned firsthand that this rule was very real.

It was about 3:00 a.m., and I was on guard duty; they always gave the FNGs the late or real early shifts. I heard a thump from a small mortar outside the perimeter and listened to the unmistakable sound of a falling mortar round.

There was an explosion with the concussion—sound, dust and confusion. By the second thump I had jumped down and was headed into the track to wake up the crew. I touched the first set of feet I could. Sgt. Ben, a former boxer, hit me square in the face and knocked me the fuck out.

When I started to come to, Sgt. Ben was dropping rounds into the deuce mortar tube and muttering under his breath. "I told that dumb motherfucker not to touch. What the fuck he thinks is goin' happen? Stupid motherfuckin' FNG." He went on and on.

They had to call and tell him to stop firing illumination rounds because they have parachutes and the helicopters could not fly with that many rounds in the air.

CHAPTER 4
If You Ain't Cavalry, You Ain't Shit

"My F---kin' Turn"

I had waited for this moment since getting in-country. We had cleaned and oiled the Ma Deuce (.50 caliber machine gun), set the head space, and were ready for our Mad Minute. We fed the belt up to the loading gate. I closed the cover and gripped the charging handle, sliding the first miniature missile of wonderful, destructive power into the chamber with a metallic clunk.

As anyone who has been defended by this destructive and powerful weapon can attest, there is a feeling of ultimate power. I felt like the most powerful being in creation. Thank you, Mr. Browning.

When you depress those butterfly triggers, to say there is a robust response would be a mass understatement. You are engulfed in concussion in your body, but your ears let you know this is raw power. Like being a dragon's voice and flames at the same time. Trees, three to ten inches in diameter, explode and fall away, clearing the view and making us feel safer. The silence that follows is deafening. Your ears ring, your body vibrates, you are shaking with adrenaline, waiting for what is next. I was now part of the club.

FRANK AND HIS MA DEUCE

We rode powerful beasts into battle, with a rumble and roar that is hard to forget. It takes you with it and the buzz never goes away. When I have had dreams or nightmares, they are of this overpowering rush and total lack of control over events. I'm feeling excited and scared to death, a powerful combination.

CHAPTER 5

Get Used to It; You Are In-Country Now!

When I boarded the plane in Cam Ranh Bay, I sat next to an ARVN trooper. He had a brand-new, shiny M1 carbine—my dream weapon. Light, fully automatic, accurate and made of wood. I found out that the US government had given these wonderful weapons to some of the worst shots and most cowardly troops in the world.

His uniform was a hodge-podge of different kinds and he wore an Aussie bush hat cocked to one side with very tight-fitting pants tucked into shined jump boots. With him was an older woman dressed like a peasant in black pajamas and a conical rice straw hat. Her teeth were purple-black. The sign: she chewed betel nut combined with lime (the mineral) in a cud-like chewing tobacco. It is a mild stimulant and it kills the pain in the teeth. There were also chickens, goats, and a potbellied pig onboard. It felt like a transport crossed with Noah's Ark. We took off with the ramp part way down—quite a rush as this was a war zone.

We flew into Pleiku Airport and were hustled to a waiting bus where the US personnel were loading. On the bus, we noticed that there was wire mesh over all of the windows and part of the windshield. When we asked about this, they told us it was "to keep them from throwing a grenade inside." This was not very comforting, and I still did not have a weapon, which sucked. I reported to the first sergeant and he sent me to the sergeant-at-arms and he lined me out for my equipment. I finally got my service weapon, an M16. It was a good weapon as long as you kept it clean. I felt a lot better but I couldn't carry it in base camp. So, I went to the E.M. Club and got drunk.

Later, I went to the shower shack and an older buck sergeant raped me and left me bruised and battered, wondering what was going to happen next.

No, I never reported it. I was a grown man; I should be able to protect myself. I shoved the rage and pain deep inside for a very long time. It helped keep me alive. I never saw the sergeant again or got a chance to take my revenge on his mortal body. I was now well armed. I joined the unit at the Oasis, a few klicks west of Pleiku.

I saw D Troop of our unit—the airmobile unit with Cobra gunships and LOHs, as well as Hueys to carry the troops. They all looked very modern in that world of ox carts and peasants with hand tools.

I am very lucky that I have a lot of the documents that document my service, starting with the induction papers from my local Draft Board #30 with the orders sending me to Vietnam.

I took some pictures with a 35mm camera I bought in the PX in base camp. I have never met with anyone that I served with in Nam, although I have communicated with some over the internet. A fellow trooper, Mr. Ron Miska from Minnesota filled in on some of the gaps. He was kind enough to send me a lot of his pictures that had me in them, and he actually remembered the names of the others in them.

The first location that I have paperwork for is from July of 1968, when B Troop left the Oasis for convoy to Ban Me Thuot, south of Pleiku. We were security for the convoy. We left mid-month and were in position for Operation Fearless, south of Ban Me Thuot in an old French rubber plantation. We where ambushed in that plantation. I was not in the lead track but was supporting in the next track. I will quote the *Ivy Leaf Famous Fourth* newspaper article dated August 25, 1968 by SP4 Obelit Yadgar.

> "Camp Enari Ivy soldiers bagged 17 NVA troops in a recent daylong operation against an estimated two-company force southwest of Ban Me Thuot.
>
> Operation Fearless was kicked off by combined forces of 4th Division as a sweep of a suspected enemy base camp near the Central Highland City.
>
> A small armored convoy of the 1st Squadron, 10th Cavalry set out on an old road to move into a blocking position, as other Ivy elements swept the area.
>
> About 10 miles south of Ban Me Thuot, a reinforced enemy platoon lay in ambush in well-camouflaged bunkers. An NVA sniper's well-aimed bullet apparently was to have been the signal to spring the ambush, as the convoy reached the kill zone.
>
> A freak accident primed the NVA to pull their ambush prematurely. They lost 12 men.
>
> A cavalryman perched on the lead armored carrier (APC). A bump on the dirt road suddenly

jolted the soldier. His rifle flew out of his grip, crashed to the ground—and discharged a round by itself.

The sniper, possibly thinking he had been detected by Ivymen, opened up with his AK-47. Then the whole line on both sides of the road burst into a screen of smoke and muzzle flash.

Bullets and rockets slammed into the road, all short of their targets, as the lead APCs fanned out and rumbled straight for the enemy, their machine guns coughing fire.

The APCs overran the enemy position, crushing their bunkers, as armed jeeps and trucks in the convoy opened up on the enemy with recoilless rifles and machine guns.

Without stopping, the APCs pulled back—and the gunships of the 7th Squadron, 17th Cavalry broke into dive after dive, riddling the enemy with miniguns and rockets. Then jets screamed in and leveled what was left of the enemy position.

The cavalrymen made a sweep of the shattered ambush site, finding three 60mm rockets, five Chicom grenades, five packs and a B-40 rocket launcher loaded and ready to fire. Gunships were called in again when the NVA fired at the convoy a mile farther up the road. But the enemy had only enough time to launch one B-40 rocket at the lead APC. The rocket missed its target. The operation

> continued, but Ivy soldiers made no further contact with the enemy.
>
> Earlier that morning however, gunships of Troop A, on a reconnaissance patrol, caught a platoon-sized enemy force in the open. Five more enemy soldiers were killed.
>
> A sweep of the area by the aero-rifle platoon yielded four NVA packs, a pistol and a radio, plus numerous documents. One NVA body was believed to be an officer."

That is the official version. Here is a different view from someone on the lead APC in this ambush.

This is from a letter I received from Mr. Ron Minska. On page 3 he states:

> "I also sent you a copy of the Ivy Leaf I saved because it was the first firefight, I was ever in. I guess it was July 1968.
>
> I think the guy who wrote it was with the 7/17 who was behind the convoy who turned back to let us fight when the 5 APCs (us) were ambushed at the head of the convoy."

CHAPTER 6
Now for the Real Story

"I remember it being an M60 on the lead APC that fired by accident, because the arms sergeant had put door gunner triggers on the M60, and it hit a branch on the trigger, which fired the first round.

I also remember that there were a lot more than 12 but they had body ropes around their waists. And their buddies came and drug off the ones in one piece during the air strikes.

I also remember Cox saving the day during the air strike because the lieutenant was too shook to get out from the steel shield to take a good compass reading, and Cox corrected him while the bombers were getting ready to dive in. If he hadn't, I wouldn't be here today. RIP Cox, the lieutenant. Got a bronze star w/v device; Cox got nothing.

I remember that 24 PC had point after the ambush when they shot the B-40 just over the top of us and it landed between 24 and 29 (my track). Then Cox (who had been shot already in the hand with an M79 by accident) nearly hit me with the 50-cal when he fired cover fire just after the B-40 missed our PC.

On page two in the 'Battle Briefs' part of the *Fighting Fourth* paper, it talked about 10th Cav. taking prisoners. Armored personnel carrier number 24 captured one NVA soldier, and I can remember holding a bead on him with the slack out of the trigger of my M60.

Peter Mainese, Track Commander of 24, got off the PC to go get him and he didn't see he was carrying an AK-47,(he started to bring him back to the PC without it). I yelled at him to take his AK-47; he didn't know he had one. It had a 30-round clip with one in the chamber. That may have been the AK in your picture.

Pete got an in-country R&R for the capture. (Rank has its privileges.) RIP

Well, I hope this does you more good than bad. I don't mind writing about it. I think that we are probably the only ones who care at all about it. It wasn't all bad; a lot of it was like a big off-road camping trip with really tough terrain and some pretty tough vehicles Ha ha!

I get a kick out of the ATTITUDE CHECK picture; I hope you do too.

Ron Miska"

I received this letter and other info plus pictures on February 17, 1997. Thanks, Ron.

Kick Em In The Guts

Here is what the unit history says about this incident:

For A/7/17 CAV
D/7/17 CAV
B/1/10 CAV
1/22 INF
For date 680729
Primary service involved, US Army
Operation MACARTHUR
Dak Lak Province, I Corps, South Vietnam
Location, Southwest Ban Me Thuot
18

Description: A/7/17 Cav reported their CO was mission command for a combined force that consisted of A and D troops, 7/17 Cav, B/1/10 Cav, D/2/35th Inf, and elements of 1/22 Inf. This force combined to make a sweep. B Troop's lead APC was hit with a B-40 rocket. D Troop deployed and returned fire with 106mm RR and AWs. The NVA withdrew to the east, carrying their dead and wounded. A Troop's scout discovered the fleeing enemy and killed 5 more. This action netted 17 NVA KIAs, 16 packs, 2 57mm RRs, 9 57mm rounds, 4 60mm motor rounds, 2 Chicom grenades, and 1 .45 cal pistol plus documents captured. The 4th Inf Div. Operation MACARTHUR report states that the CO of A/7/17 Cav commanded TASK FORCE FEARLESS, which conducted a raid on a suspected enemy base area and arms cache on Chu Ta Ting, one of the hills southwest of Ban Me Thuot near the Ea Krong River. D/7/17 Cav (Motorized) and B/1/10 Cav rolled overland to establish blocking positions northwest and northeast of objective. B/5/16th Arty (155SP) and two eight-inch Howitzers of B/5/22 Arty moved to site at ZU190950, where Route 14 crosses the Ea Krong River. At 1145, they opened fire to prepare LZs for infantry assault force. At about 1205, while ascending the main ridge south of Ban Me Thuot AU246895), APCs of B/1/10 came under fire from an estimated reinforced platoon in a bunker complex. Employing 57mm RRs and small arms, the enemy damaged one APC and wounded one crewman. Returning fire with .50 caliber 106mm RRs, artillery, and gunship support, the cavalry silenced the enemy positions. Helleborine CAs to LZs south of Chu Ta Ting began shortly after noon. While preparing the infantry's primary LZ, A/7/17th Cav gunships received ground to air fire. They returned fire on enemy positions, killing five NVA; the lift ships carrying D/3/35 Inf diverted to an alternate LZ at ZU224863, 1300 meters southwest of Chu Ta Ting. They discovered nothing of significance. During the afternoon, D/7/17 Cav explored the area of contact, finding a complex of 40 bunkers and 12 NVA KIA. Two of the bodies were booby-trapped with 60mm motor rounds and one was booby-trapped with a satchel charge. Additionally, they found two 57mm RR's, one AN/GRC-9 radio, one US .45 cal pistol, two AK-47s and an eight-inch stack of documents. Readout of documents identified the K39NVA Bn.

MIKE WITH AK-47

FRANK WITH AK-47

CAPTURED WEAPONS

PRISONER

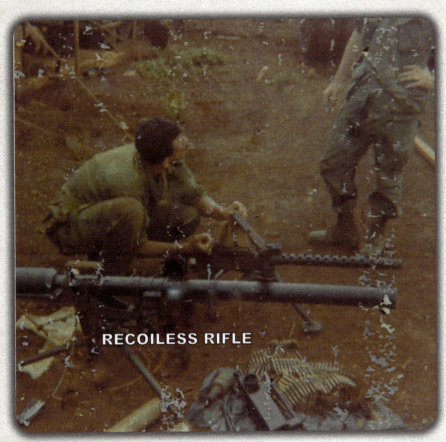

RECOILLESS RIFLE

CHAPTER 7
Mistakes Can Kill Ya

I remember the closest call I had in Vietnam. I was driving. We were a blocking force for an infantry sweep in coordination with a B-52 strike. We were with 35th Infantry.

There were men spread along a line with tanks (M48 Sheridans) and tracks (M113s). As we were traveling along, there was a small tree with some sparse bushes up ahead. The TC told me to put the tree close to the left side of the track.

As we drove past, out of the corner of my eye, I spotted some movement. A straw mat was lifted and an AK-47 was being pointed and fired. I felt the first-round impact of the APC with a loud report and shock waves. I instantly dropped into the safety of the track.

While I dropped, I pulled the left lateral hard right and listened as the Ma Deuce did her job. The man was cut in half by the .50 caliber rounds.

He had fired a full magazine of 30 rounds and hit no one. He had walked his rounds up across to where I was sitting. He broke two of the periscopes and cut off two antennae but did not hit any of us.

We recovered the AK-47, and there is a picture of me and another trooper holding it; men must have their trophies. The man was old and had malaria and dysentery. He had given his life to give his buddies some time—brave but fatal.

Sometime around this time, another accident almost caused my death.

In Vietnam, when they refuel a track or a tank in the field, they don't like to make a lot of noise by using a loud pump, so, they have the engineers dig a big, deep pit (for the tracks, 7-8 feet deep, and the tanks, 10-12 feet deep) to drive into, then the refueling truck just has to open up the tap and gravity takes over; silent.

Our platoon had just refueled in the afternoon and moved off a few klicks to set up our perimeter. We set out the concertina wire; every track had a few coils and we put out our trip flares and sent out our ambushes and listening posts.

In Vietnam, it got dark really quick. It was about 0330 hours when the ambush reported a lot of movement by the enemy and that they sounded scared over the radio. Then there were a few scattered shots and a trip flare went off in the distance in the vicinity of the ambush.

Our lieutenant, a recent graduate of West Point (in a class of 56, he was #56), decided against all logic to go out and rescue them with our tacks, using the night vision Starlight scopes.

I was driving again. We headed toward the ambush site—not in a column but spread in a line, moving forward toward the ambush. We hadn't gone far when I found the refueling pit.

The APC plunged headfirst into the deepest part of the hole. All was confusion. I remember I was driving the mortar track, full of live Four-Deuce rounds (about 105 mm), into the refueling pit.

I was knocked out, as was the TC. The engine screamed like a wounded animal. The rescue was called off. Now we had to be rescued.

We were pulled to safety and the TC had to be airlifted to the aid station. He broke his collarbone and dislocated his shoulder. He rejoined us about a month later.

After Operation Fearless, we moved north to secure Highway 14 to Pleiku, and then on to the LZ Oasis to refit.

We had contact on September 5, 1968, with one KIA, and we were ambushed again on September with nine WIA.

On October 12, 1968, we hit a mine with one WIA, and we returned to Ban Me Thuot on October 31, 1968, and stayed there until I went on R&R to Hong Kong, November 14, 1968, and returned November 19, 1968.

We then left to travel north to the Oasis, 12km SW of Pleiku, near the Catecka Tea Plantation.

Our unit traveled north to Kon Tum and were back at the Oasis on December 6, 1968, then North again to Kon Tum and stayed there, securing a bridge and an artillery unit, until January 17, 1968, when we returned to the Oasis to refit. By February 1, 1968, we were at Plei Djereng SF Camp, also known as Le Minh Camp, as security.

We traveled to the SE Song River. I waded across it and set up an ambush; unfortunately, it was very successful and a very sad thing to see or be part of. I carry many ugly scars with me, but they are mine. I earned them, damn it.

February 18, 1968, we were at LZ Lanetta, then we returned to the Oasis.

On March 2, 1968, at 0955 hours, the track I was on hit a buried 175mm shell and I was thrown 30 feet into the air. When I landed, I dislocated my left hip.

I was dusted off to the 4th Evac Hospital. I returned to the unit at the Oasis on March 6,1968, and I received my Purple Heart in the field, March, 9, 1968.

Then I began to have headaches and vomiting on March 19. I fainted and had a grand mal seizure and was finally on my way home.

CHAPTER 8
The Best Damn Monkey Story

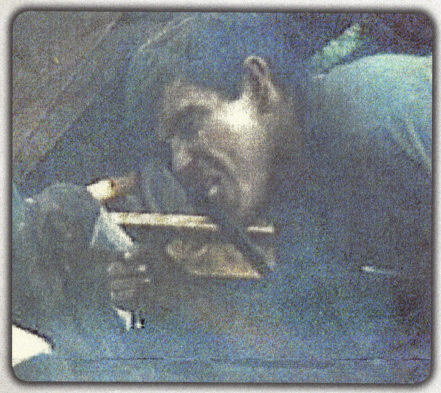

ME AND MY MONKEY

When you are crashing bush with an APC, you learn a lot about what lives in the tops of bamboo thickets when you ram them.

Whatever is in the top falls into the top opening of the M113A1—this included all sorts of insects and spiders—but the thing we feared the most was the "two-step snake," AKA the bamboo viper. It was long and bright green, and like the name says, it was poisonous. Talking with some of the older guys about our problem, we were told we should buy a monkey—one of the macaque tailless monkeys that lived in the Central Highlands.

Soon, we were outside a Mountain Yard village and a man had a monkey for sale; I knew he was a good monkey as he had pierced ears. I traded two cases of C-rations for him.

We rigged up a long lead out of parachute cord and tied it to our tallest antenna, allowing him to reach any part of the track.

He got very excited when we were crashing bush because he ate all the bugs and spiders that fell into our track. He would dance around and make the most robust sounds while chewing the heads off scary big bugs. He really got excited when a small four-foot python fell in; he went "ape shit." He was upset for days after we threw it out.

He had a habit that all of us boys found endearing. Whenever he could, he would handle his package—very casually and with a nonchalant manner. We all admired that about it.

We were at the Oasis when it happened: Our troop was standing down for regular maintenance, and there were six or seven of us standing around the APC, when we looked up and saw a "Donut Dolly," waving and coming our way.

We were all dumbfounded as we had not seen a round-eyed chick in months.

She was full on 1960s: teased blond hair with bangs that didn't move because of the hairspray. But the one thing we all noticed were her tits; they were very Dolly Parton in size and we were all transfixed, staring with unabashed lust as she asked, "Where are you from? How are you?"

As we watched her bounce and wiggle, no one was watching the monkey.

She had backed up to within a few feet of the APC, which was about seven feet off the ground. The monkey was perched on the edge of the track, about to leap into action.

Without warning, he launched himself onto the girl's blond hairdo and began to rhythmically hump her head in a very vigorous and frantic way that we all knew was monkey love!

We were breathless with laughter, tears streaming down our cheeks, helplessly watching as our blonde angel screamed and began to run. The leash was 20 feet long and the antenna was about 15 feet, so she ran about 35 feet at full speed. When the rope went taut, my monkey was jerked from his blonde monkey love to be slammed to the ground.

When I got to him, I swear he had a slight smile and was still flinching and wiggling. I gently picked him up and carried him back in triumph.

For days after, people stopped by to see "the monkey who got some head" and brought him bananas.

That is not the end of the story.

When I was living in Washington in about 1995, I was shopping at a Fred Meyer store in Everett. A woman stopped me and noticed that I was a Vietnam veteran (I was wearing a vet's cap).

"Which unit were you with in Vietnam?" she asked me.

"Tenth Armored Cavalry," I replied.

"That was the last unit I visited when I was a Donut Dolly."

I was dumbstruck; I could see her as a blonde all those years ago, running for her life. I asked no more questions. I did not want to do any more harm.

Some monkeys should be left alone!

CHAPTER 9

But They Are on Our Side, Aren't They?

The next adventure that I remember happened after the ambush in the rubber plantation south of Ban Me Thuot.

When we arrived at the base, the ARVN troopers were just pulling their tracks out; they did not want to go fight. We heard "hot chow" was being served at the mess hall, since we had not had a hot meal in over a week. We headed for the chow hall, and when we arrived, we did not have our covers (hats).

So, we headed back to the track to get them. As I came in sight of our track, I saw an ARVN stealing our C-rations off the top of our APC.

I yelled and he ran out into the berm area in front of the track. I caught him and grabbed him by the shoulder and turned around as Cassell Lewis knocked him out. Then we heard the unmistakable sound of weapons being charged with live rounds. We turned around to face six pissed-off ARVNs with loaded guns pointed at us.

We let the thief go. Just then, we heard a voice speaking Vietnamese really loud, which is unusual in their culture.

The ARVN troops went to parade rest. We were not going to die today.

The voice belonged to the Vietnamese first sergeant who was pissed—not at us, but at his trooper. He had stolen from a guest in their country, fighting for their freedom.

As we watched, he had the thief go out into the bush and cut a branch the size of his middle finger, about three feet long.

We watched as the first sergeant made the thief strip to the waist, as his friends watched. Then the first sergeant beat him on the face and shoulders. Angry red welts rose with each stroke.

By the fourth or fifth stroke, I wanted to give the man the C-rations. I was beginning to feel the blows. I do not know long it lasted, but it was long and uncomfortable.

Through an interpreter, the first sergeant apologized and said he would make it up to us.

We went to chow, wondering "WTF?" over and over.

Later that night, the first sergeant sent for us. We went to his very nice bunker; he had invited us to a feast. We ate barbecue monkey meat and lots of other stuff (I still don't know exactly what it was). He also had a "Boom Boom girl" for us (a hooker). We both enjoyed her company and talents. The first sergeant's family lived in Ban Me Thuot, and they owned the hotel—the tallest building in town (three stories tall with a basement opium den). The first sergeant talked to our captain and got permission for us to go into town with the first sergeant. We sampled all of the delights of the brothel, hotel, restaurant, bar and opium den with equal gusto.

I will not bore or offend anyone with the tawdry details; besides, some of the women could still be alive, and I would never wish to offend a lady of the night—one never knows when you may need one.

We stayed out until the first sergeant informed us that we had to leave because the NVA were coming that evening to do just what we were doing. And would pay.

The first sergeant explained that he had to live here after we were gone. And he was a businessman, so he needed to provide the local troops, both North and South, with a bribe. We left tired and proud to have had some very interesting experiences.

We spent two days sleeping after that. The captain never asked about our absence, and we provided no details. It was a wonderful respite from the terror and fear.

When I joined the unit at the Oasis, there was a young Vietnamese boy of about 10 or 11 there. His name was, of course, Joe. When I asked about Joe, this is what I was told.

"Little Joe's Story"

When our unit was going through Joe's village, our unit was ambushed, and when they rounded up the villagers to ask who had done it, Joe came forward and pointed out the Viet Cong, and they were taken away. That night, the Viet Cong came back and killed his parents and siblings, and he barely got away with his life.

He found his way to our unit, and through an interpreter, he told the captain what had happened.

The captain took him in as our mascot.

Kick Em In The Guts

When I joined the unit, Joe was already part of the unit. He wore our used fatigues. He was one of the best checkers and chess players I've ever lost to; we all played him and we all lost. He was saving money to buy guns for his village, so, naturally, we wanted to help him.

Joe was around for a few months, and then one day he was gone. Along with all his stuff and savings. We all wondered where he had disappeared.

Then one day when we were going on a chow run, we looked up, and standing in the middle of the road was Joe and a group of armed urchins, yelling and waving their arms to stop us. Joe and his mini army had been on the way to a US dump to scavenge for stuff to sell when one of the small boys stepped on a mine buried in the ground. But he was not heavy enough to trigger it. The enemy had set them for our tracks.

The new lieutenant did not know Joe and was very angry and very scared. We explained the situation.

Joe went on to show us four more mines: all were 175mm artillery shells we had left behind or were duds. They would have destroyed our tracks.

We asked Joe what he wanted for saving our lives. All he wanted was a case or two of C-rations and some ammunition for his few weapons.

Our lieutenant absolutely forbid us to give this "gook" kid anything and ordered us to mount up and move out.

I personally gathered up as many .30 caliber rounds as I could and put them in a small bag and threw them to Joe. I then watched as track after track kicked off cases of

C-rations in thanks for their lives. What were they going to do to me? Send me to Vietnam? Whoops, too late.

I never saw Joe again or heard anything further about him. I sure hope he is okay. I never got to properly thank him for saving all of our lives. Thanks again, Joe.

As a lot of books and movies have pointed out, there were very distinct groups among us. The "lifers" (career soldiers; usually gung ho) generally drank a lot of booze.

The "heads" were mostly draftees, not career oriented, just trying to make it through the year. I was in this group. We usually smoked pot. Then there were the "rednecks," "hillbillies," and "shitkickers"—they could go either way; some drank and some smoked.

"A Career of Whore Inspections"

And then there were the "brothers"—the Black soldiers, most of whom had been drafted—and I learned a lot from them. I was an honorary brother, for one reason and one reason only. When I arrived in Vietnam, I had just been dropped by my girlfriend. So, I was completely free of any and all commitments, and I soon found that my new situation was ripe for many, many sexual adventures.

In Utah, if you wanted sex, you had to marry the girl and do the old courtship dance, promising to be true forever. I had tried that.

I discovered that in Vietnam you could trade money for sex.

What a concept. Easy and simple, it was an exchange and no other nonsense. As soon as this service was presented to me, I wholeheartedly took part in this new capitalist experiment. Every chance I got, I would slip off to the whore houses, and every time we stopped, I would find a Boom Boom girl and indulge in my favorite pastime.

"Son, you would fuck a snake if someone would hold the head!" said the first sergeant as I passed his track.

An example of my behavior:

We were waiting on the highway to escort a convoy to Ban Me Thuot, when I spied a Boom Boom girl, so I jumped off the track and headed across the road for some recon. The TC (track commander) yelled at me and asked me, "Where the hell you goin', Sky Pilot?" But when he saw the Boom Boom girl, he just motioned for me to continue. He knew that I had a mission.

The brothers approached me to talk to me about my nocturnal forays. They had noticed that I was very sexually active and I never caught any VDs. They wanted to know my secret.

I told them it was simple; I had rules. And here they are:

1) You never pick the best-looking or the ugliest girl; always pick the mid-range. Unless there is just one, then you are limited in your choice.

2) Always wash your penis off; I have used everything from Jim Beam whiskey to Shasta cream soda.

Jim Beam burns a little.

Shasta cream soda makes it sticky.

They decided that while I was on their track, they wouldn't have sex with anyone until I had cleared the way. It was an awesome responsibility, but I took it seriously. It meant a lot of extra recon to keep my brothers safe. Yeah, I was a dick.

I recently found a blue plastic photo album with the flag of Vietnam on the cover. Inside, I found a lot of pictures and memorabilia from my year. There were a lot of pictures of Vietnamese girls who I do not remember.

VIETNAMESE LADIES CIRCA 1968

FRANK AND IREANE 1968

Only one photo had a name attached to it, and it was not a Vietnamese name but "Leslie." There were a total of seven pictures, with a total of eight unknown women in them who knew me well enough to give me a picture.

CHAPTER 10
There Are Traps Everywhere

I went on R&R from Nov. 14, 1968, to Nov. 19, 1968. I wanted to go to Australia but all of those slots were filled by REMFs (rear echelon motherfuckers).

So, I chose Hong Kong. I flew in from the Oasis then flew to Cam Ranh Bay. That afternoon, I took a bus to the beach and, on the way, a tire blew and it sounded just like an AK-47 and everyone who was a field trooper hit the deck and crawled under the seats.

The rest of the base camp commandos looked at us like we were crazy. I still don't like loud noises. We may have lost some pride but we were still alive.

Then we flew off to Hong Kong, a short hop.

We landed and I really thought that we were going to land in someone's living room. The old Hong Kong airport was really something to fly into and out of. They built a whole island for the new airport.

"Now, Have a Good Time with the Ladies"

Once we touched down, we were hustled off to the all-important venereal disease presentation. It was presented by very serious men in starched and shined uniforms and boots.

Then they showed us the most GOD-AWFUL film, consisting of every conceivable venereal disease and their ominous warning:

"If you catch the Black Syphilis, they will lock you up on a hospital ship, and tell your family you were KIA. Now, have a good time with ladies." The sadistic bastards just smiled through perfect teeth.

I checked into the Hong Kong Hilton Hotel; it was by far the best hotel I had ever been in. I was in awe. When I stepped off the elevator on the fourth floor, a Chinese man greeted me in perfect English as I exited the elevator:

"Hello, sir. My name is Winston and I have been assigned to be your butler while you are here."

He reached down and took my bag, took my key and unlocked my door.

Now I had seen some great service but this was a step above. He took my clothes and expertly folded them into the drawers.

He then turned to me and asked, "What would you like to do in Hong Kong, sir?" I told him I was in town to buy some custom-made suits and some camera gear.

"Very good, sir. If you would follow me to the lobby, we can begin shopping." He opened the door and we went to the elevator and descended to the lobby.

When we exited, I headed for the main doors. Winston shouted and motioned me toward a small side door.

Something set off all of my well-tuned instincts; something was wrong here. I went to the door and peered around the corner. I saw a large German car and some of the biggest Chinese guys I had ever seen. I dove back into the lobby and ran to the front desk to report what had happened.

I found out later that the Tongs were trying to kidnap American servicemen and sell them to the North Vietnamese as prisoners.

I did buy a lot of clothes, including a pure white silk-and-wool Nehru suit with wide bell-bottom pants, and a turquoise turtleneck with a large silver-and-turquoise stone to wear around my neck.

"Real Estate in Hong Kong"

The most interesting thing happened on the last day. I got a call on the house phone, and on the other end was a very pleasant female voice with a delightful English accent.

"You have been selected to attend a cultural event," she said.

I, of course, heard, "Would you please come have sex with me?" in my poor, demented 19-year-old mind. Naturally, I accepted.

When I arrived in the lobby, there were two other GIs, so I thought it was going to be group sex . . . wrong again. We were ushered into a limousine and taken to a fancy hotel in downtown Hong Kong, where the top floor overlooked the cultural event.

We were seated at a long table with room for at least ten people per side. On one side, sat the GIs and the other very well-dressed men. Then they brought in a group of dancing girls with Thai costumes.

They danced for a few minutes, and then they got down to business.

The man who was sitting across from me had a bright red dot in the middle of his forehead. He was Indian.

"Sir, you have a golden opportunity to make a fortune today. If you invest today, you could double or triple your money very quickly," he said.

Mr. Bobo (honest to God, that was his name) then told me his wonderful opportunity was undeveloped land in South Florida. That's right, folks; they were trying to sell me swampland in Florida. I was dumbfounded. The room erupted in applause as one of the GIs signed the papers. They all yelled and clapped and slapped him on the back.

I sat there and thought how fucking unreal this all was, and then I started to laugh long and hard.

"You have got to be fucking kidding me. Fuck you all!" I said. I was unceremoniously escorted to the street. This world can be very strange.

I never did get any sex, but what a lesson. I was almost relieved to return to the bush. At least the rules were simple there. Just survive one more day.

CHAPTER 11
Mud in Ban Me Thuot

Mud in Ban Me Thuot

Cox

In Ban Me Thuot, during the monsoon, I jumped off of the APC and got stuck in the thick red mud and it pulled off my boots.

We were building a mortar pit when our TC (track commander), Duane Cox (RIP), began yelling at Cassell Lewis, which was unusual because Cox was always cool and calm. Soon they were fist-fighting all over the mortar pit. We tried to separate them.

I found out later that it was all an act to embarrass the captain.

MISKA WITH MORTAR TUBE

MORTAR TRACK HOME FOR 9 MONTHS

JIM BRYANT PLACING A CLAYMORE MINE

TED COLFER

SIR, OUR FAVORITE LT.

BOXIE

PLATOON SERGEANT ROY YOUNG

RON MISKA

JEFF, DARRELL AND COLFER

THE BLOND TANKER, JERRY COLE

BOXIE AND MISKA

PORK A.K.A. GARY RUTTER AND DARRELL COLE

LT. PLUMBER & DOC

FRANK STEPHENS, GARY RUTTER AND UNKNOWN

ATTITUDE CHECK

TRIBAL SOLDIER

TRIBAL BURIAL

B-TROOP ASCENDS HILL-TRACK

B-TROOP ASCENDS HILL-TANK

ME ACTING COOL

SE SONG RIVER, KON TOM, VIETNAM

MIKE HAGER

Christmas 1968, LZ Oasis

Wounded

We were on our way to pick up hot chow for our unit and I was riding beside the TC on my lawn chair (for comfort and cool), with my goggles, steel pot, flak jacket and M16 ready for action when it happened.

Our track hit a large land mine On March 2, 1969. We were lifted high into the air as the violent explosion that we set off tore the world around us to shreds. The roar of the explosion echoes in my ears to this day—I still don't hear well. I remember reaching out for my rifle; I was going to punish someone for this. That thought was blasted from my head when I came down from almost 30 feet in the air. I landed on some large rocks and dislocated my left hip. (I now have a new metal one.) I lost consciousness for a while.

The first thing I remember was one of the "heads" asking me for my stash; they would Article 15 you if they found pot on you. I motioned to my cargo pocket and he took it and left. The next to appear was our medic. He was a conscious objector and he would not carry a weapon, ever. He was the bravest man I ever met. He asked if I was in pain . . . I was! He then hit me with a dose of morphine. WOW. I had never felt anything like that in my life. The world faded away and I was high. I vaguely remember being carried to the dust-off flight.

CHAPTER 12
Dusted Off

DUST-OFF

When I returned to the States, it was not in a victory parade.

I saw the ground fall away while the rotor roared overhead. When we arrived at the aid station, they asked me what was wrong with me and I said, "Not a fucking thing," and tried to walk into the station. I fell flat on my face. Morphine is strong stuff.

They never dealt with the concussion I received on that day; it was part of the cause of my seizure.

I stayed in the hospital for two days and returned to my unit, now at the Oasis on a stand-down. I had gotten a bad cold in the hospital and they gave me some horse-sized antibiotics capsules.

I went out in the sun and helped stretch more concertina wire around the perimeter. Then I had a grand mal seizure. It happened at Oasis Base Camp on March 21, 1969 at 1325 hours. When I woke up, I had two IVs in my arms and a medic leaning over me and saying in a calm voice, "You are going home now." The words I had been waiting to hear. I slept.

These are the facts as I know them, and I have the documents to prove that they happened.

"Headed Home"

I was transferred from 8th Field Hospital to 71st Evacuation Hospital.

I went through Cam Rahn Bay and was flown to Japan via a Marine Corps Medevac flight to Hokkaido, Japan. On the flight I was witness to something that has stayed with me all these years.

Frank O Stephens

The bunks were very close together and you could hear and feel a lot of what went on. As a BAM (pardon me, ladies, big-assed Marine—the female Marine Corps nurses) nurse leaned in, the wounded lieutenant above me grabbed her boob. I felt her stiffen, getting ready for the next move. As he increased his pressure, the nurse slid her hand down to his nuts and grabbed them hard. He shuddered as her expert grip brought him to a brutal reality: HE HAD FUCKED UP! She continued to exert her pressure to let him know who was in control.

Then she leaned in to his face and almost whispered, "Now then, sir, that will be enough of that." And then she twisted harder as he grunted out loud.

It was at that point that I noticed I was holding on to my own nuts.

Whenever that nurse went by, I would tuck my hands well away. I went to Travis Air Force Base and had my first steak in a long time and a long, long shower.

The red dirt of Nam was everywhere and I really enjoyed flushing the toilet . . . WOW, running water, both hot and cold! I found this old printed letter I sent home from Vietnam late in my tour, September or October of 1968.

The really sad thing about this letter is it was printed out and distributed to us as a clever tongue-in-cheek, humorous letter, so the folks back home could have a laugh. It sadly foretells my future, never to be the same life.

> "Dear civilians, friends, draft dodgers, etc. In the very near future, the undersigned will once more be in your midst, dehydrated and demoralized, to take his place again as a human being with the well-known forms of

freedom and justice for all, and to engage in life, liberty and the somewhat delayed pursuit of happiness. In making joyous preparations to welcome him back into organized society, you might take certain steps to make allowances for the past twelve months.

In other words, he might be a little Asiatic from Vietnamesitis and Overseasitis, and should be handled with care. Don't be alarmed if he is infested with all forms of rare tropical disease. A little time in the Land of the Big PX will cure this malady.

Therefore, show no alarm if he insists on carrying a weapon to the dinner table, looks around for his steel pot when offered a chair, or wakes you in the middle of the night for guard duty.

Keep cool when he pours gravy on his dessert at dinner or mixes peaches with his Seagram's VO.

Pretend not to notice if he acts dazed, eats with his fingers instead of silverware, and prefers C-rations to steak.

Take it with a smile when he insists on digging up the garden to fill sandbags for the bunker he is building.

Be tolerant when he takes his blanket and sheet off the bed and puts them on the floor to sleep.

Abstain from saying anything about powdered eggs, dehydrated potatoes, fried rice, fresh milk, or ice cream.

Do not be alarmed if he should jump up from the dinner table and rush to the garbage can and wash his plate with a toilet brush. After all, this has been his standard.

Also, if it should start raining, pay no attention to him if he pulls off his clothes, grabs a bar of soap and a towel and runs outside for a shower.

When, in his daily conversation, he utters such things as: 'Xin Loi' and 'Choi Oi,' just be patient, and simply leave quickly and calmly if by some chance he utters, 'Di Di' with an irritated look on his face because it means no less than 'Get the hell out of here.'

Do not let it shake you up if he picks up the phone and yells, 'Sky King forward, sir,' or says, 'Roger out' for goodbye, or simply shouts, 'Working!'

Never ask why the Jones boy held a higher rank than he did, and by no means mention the word 'extend.'

Pretend not to notice if, at a restaurant, he calls the waitress 'Number One Girl,' and uses his hat as an ashtray.

He will probably keep listening for 'Homeward bound' to sound off over AFRS. If he does, comfort him, for he is still reminiscing.

Be especially watchful when he is in the presence of a woman—especially a beautiful woman.

Above all, keep in mind that beneath that tanned and rugged exterior, there is a heart of gold (the only thing of value he has left). Treat him with kindness, tolerance, and an occasional fifth of good liquor and you will be able to rehabilitate that which was once (and is now a hollow shell) the happy-go-lucky guy you loved.

Last, but not least, send no more money to the APO, fill the icebox with beer, get the civvies out of the mothballs, fill the car with gas, and get the women and children off the streets . . . BECAUSE THE KID IS COMING HOME!!!!!!

[Signed with my signature]"

On the other side is a hand written note saying:

"I will be stationed at Fort Carson, Colorado, 2 BN, 11 Inf. We have been in a lot of action lately, that's why I haven't written more often. We got to go out again. I'll see you soon. I want to buy a new car about the first week I'm home: TR-6, good deal. $3200-$3400. I like them.

Your Son, Frank."

This letter made me very sad because it was foretelling the truth; we just thought it was clever and sarcastic and in-your-face. It was a symbol for my Vietnam experience. I cannot and will not speak for any other veterans, except for including the written records of a very few of my fellow troopers. I have their permission to share our history.

I have two more letters from that era of my life.

One is not dated but was sent from Fort Knox, Kentucky, when I was in AIT. It reads:

> "Dear Mom & Dad,
>
> Well, another week and weekend have slipped away and also another pay day. I got paid $81.00 this month. Last month I got $68.00. This month I got $20.00 for food when I was on Christmas leave. Next month I expect about $68.00 again, but I will be E-2 the 15th of March (1968), then I get $106.00 before everything is taken out—and if I'm lucky, I will get PFC when I get out of AIT (I hope). We had a big inspection Saturday and my squad and our room looked the best in the whole platoon. (Pretty good?)
>
> I got the iron and Grandma's bread and jam. Thank you both very much for both. It really tasted good.
>
> Mike [my older brother] wrote me and told me about Linda's visit, and I think he is finally starting to appreciate just what he's got. I think he is finally growing up (funny me talking about my big brother like that).
>
> I am sending you $20.00. I will keep the rest to buy things.

I will get you a spoon as soon as I get to town [my mom collected small spoons—I told you I am a mommy's boy].

Tell Grandmother and Grandfather I miss them very much and I even wish I were home to cut their lawn (I will be in a while; right now, I think I'm the luckiest man alive. Everyone around here spends money on cigarettes, booze and some even have dope)."

This is the earliest mention of drugs in my records.

"And, you know, I thought I would be tempted, but because of my faith [having been born and raised a Mormon] and my blessing [a patriarchal blessing given by a Mormon church high official; his name was Mr. Pace of Coalville, Utah] I'm not at all. I've got a healthy body and an alert mind—Why mess them up? I thank God every night for my blessings. [That's pretty good for me.] I still haven't found an LDS ward. But I'm still looking.

Well, goodbye for now. I miss you both very much. I hope you have a lot of (triplets). (Lambs)

See you soon.

Your loving son, Frank"

The next and only other letter from Vietnam, is on Red Cross stationery and reads:

> "March 26, 1969
>
> Dear Mom & Dad,
>
> Well I've got some good news (finally). I'm on my way HOME. Right now, I'm in the 8th Field Hospital in Na Trang, and tomorrow I will go to Cam Rahn Bay, then to Japan and from there, the States, then home.
>
> They don't know what is wrong with me; I passed out and had some sort of seizure (I shook all over. I know what caused it, but I won't tell until I get home). So I should be home sooner than I figured. At least I will be where they don't shoot at me. So, I'll let you know more later.
>
> Your homeward-bound son, Frank"

I signed this one with a peace sign in the corner. I was two polar opposites: one young and carefree, and the other, jaded and wounded in body and spirt.

This is just part of the overall story of my life. I have been married twice and nursed the woman I loved for 37 years till the day she died in my arms. I have known great loss and great joy.

I have been extremely lucky to have done and seen all the things I have. I began revisiting Vietnam as soon as the Vietnamese would allow us back in. We had a bad record with them.

Kick Em In The Guts

In 2000, my wife and I took our first trip to Vietnam, post-conflict. We went with a Canadian tour company. Our guides were an Indonesian-Canadian and an ex-South Vietnamese sergeant.

Once Nam (the ex-South Vietnamese solider) learned that I had been in the US Army in Vietnam, he instantly took a liking to me and brought me things to eat that he not would allow the rest of the group to eat.

"Because you were here once, so you can handle it," was all he said.

VILLAGE CHILD APRIL 2000

"THE HEALING TOUCH, OF A CHILD."

We were on a tour in Hue, up the Perfume River, touring a village where they make conical hats, and I was still jumpy and a little ill at ease.

Then a small boy of about two or three, who was wearing his red-and-blue-striped polo shirt inside out and backwards, came up to me and grabbed the two outside fingers of my left hand. Somehow, that little boy's touch let decades of rage, fear and anger subside and I began to cry. He led me around his village for some time. I was not aware of the time passing, just the relief of the burden gone.

I have a picture of the little boy, but he will never know how much his touch allowed to happen.

TRONG AND FAMILY 2019

In Hoi An, I met a young man of about 18, and in my heart I adopted him. I have now known him for 17 years. I knew that I couldn't help rebuild the whole country, but I could help this one young man.

Today, my son has two fine sons of his own. He lives with and takes care of his aging parents and manages restaurants for a major Asian hotel chain. I have gone back almost every year to see him, at least 14 times in all.

I spend at least one month, but preferably two months, with my Vietnamese family.

I have traveled to Vietnam to exorcise my own demons from the war. After my first trip, I stayed in touch with Trong. My adopted son was working for his aunt In Hoi An in Quang Nam Province, about 30km from Da Nang in the central part of Vietnam.

At first, I helped him with a few dollars per month ($5.00-$10.00 per month) so he could go to school, which he did, and his English improved much faster than my Vietnamese.

By my third or fourth trip in the 2007-2009 time frame, Trong married Le and he had his first son, James (not his real name). Almost all Vietnamese take some sort of nickname that Westerners can pronounce. And then, six years later, they had Ben, the youngest of my grandchildren.

On my first few trips, I visited the places where I had been stationed. I also got to see Dalat, Na Trang, and Ban Me Thuot, which was kind of spooky for me. My body remembered and the hair on the back of my neck stood on end.

This continues until today. On our trip before last, my son took us on a drive, and we took a shortcut, got lost and ended up at the Dak To airport, where I had been in a firefight almost 40 years ago and my body still remembered. It was hard for me to explain my discomfort.

I plan to continue to visit Vietnam as often as I can for as long as I can.

Frank O Stephens

I was watching an episode of CNN's *Parts Unknown with Anthony Bourdain*, featuring president Barack Obama, and they said in essence that Vietnam was the benchmark for fuck-ups in history. This pisses me off; they are sitting there, eating a bowl of soup, 50 years after the supposed fuck-up, in a rapidly growing capitalist country that did it without our help.

How long do they think it will take us to be that comfortable? In, let's say, Beirut, Syria or the whole Middle East, which Obama didn't help.

I have heard about the Greatest Generation from Tom Brokaw. My dad was a good man, but he used to get drunk and abuse us, so they were just people.

If they are the Greatest Generation, where do we, Vietnam veterans, fit? I did what they did, except the average Vietnam veteran saw more prolonged combat than any WWII outfit. And we smoked pot while doing it—take that, Greatest Generation.

CHAPTER 13
My Welcome Home

From Travis AFB in California we flew to Mountain Home AFB, Idaho, where I got my one and only parade. I looked up from the stretcher, and coming up the open ramp was a little old lady and she gave everyone on the flight a hot dog with a small American flag stuck in it. No catsup, mustard or onions— they just gave you the plain wiener, well inserted.

My final destination was Fitzsimmons General Army Hospital in Aurora, Colorado. It was the closest military hospital to my hometown of Henefer, Utah.

I was in the hospital and being treated by April 1, 1969. I was treated for internal parasites, a seizure disorder. I was given Dilantin and all I did was sleep.

After my initial treatment, my doctor, a major, told me, "Go to the outpatient barracks and stay out of sight."

I was very good at that already. "Yes, sir."

In less than a week, I requested and received a weekend leave to go home for the first time.

I flew to SLC Utah, and my mother and stepfather met me at the airport. Our family had never been very loving; no hugging, just a strong handshake. They were glad to see me but guarded.

I was sooo quiet.

The next day I went to Weber State College and took my SATs for college entrance.

I arrived very early and sat in the very back corner of the room, wearing my field jacket and my boonie hat pulled over my face, trying to hide. I did not do well on the tests.

I sat and listened to the other young people complain about their new cars and clothes.

I knew that at that very moment, across the ocean in Vietnam, boys their age were dying.

I wanted to cry and scream, but it would do no good. That began my new life of quiet rage, anger and self-destructive behavior.

I returned to the hospital because I was still in the army. I went off campus (base) or off the hospital grounds and started to find my way around.

I soon had a girlfriend who was a real stoner, and so I had weed.

"Weed Riot"

Just after I arrived and got settled in, the guys from Hamburger Hill started to roll in. I say that because the NVA had set their guns to wound the most men they could; it takes three men out of action if they have to carry you.

Kick Em In The Guts

Most of these guys were tore up and hurting in ways you or I hopefully will never know. I got to know a few of them, and they all had one need: weed. Wow, what a coincidence because I could get some. I would have it for them the next day, out back by the trees and smokestack.

We began an informal group of convulsing combat vets who met in the afternoon and talked shit and smoked hard. This went on for a few weeks, and then one afternoon it went south fast.

It was a Friday night and I was holding the bowl for a guy who couldn't use his hands yet. Then I heard, "Stop that right now and hand me the marijuana!" Now, this should have scared me, but I was really stoned and we never called it that, so it sounded funny and I laughed.

The last thing an MP expects is to be laughed at, and when I looked up and over, I saw a very pissed and advancing young military policeman intent on arresting me.

FUCK. What now?

I was standing next to a guy who had only one arm left and he tugged at my shirt and asked me to give him the grass. I complied and he took it and tucked it under his stump of a body.

When the MP reached our circle, the men were wheeling their chairs to get in his way, so he got pissed at me—the only semi-whole body there. He asked me to give him the dope and I told him I did not have it.

One guy in a wheelchair said, "Why don't you try searching a cripple? Or are you scared?"

That is when that young MP made a big mistake: he grabbed a combat vet. These men had just been through more hell than anyone I have ever known and now they could vent some of their anger. These wounded men grabbed that young MP and dragged him to the ground and started pounding on him. They were a fighting unit again!

It was ugly and beautiful at the same time. I had retrieved the baggie and dumped it as soon as I could, so when the orderlies started to arrive, all they saw was an MP wrestling with men who were out of their wheelchairs and some of them had IV drips that had been torn out.

What was going on?

The MP got in some trouble over that; we heard they sent him to Vietnam.

In the next few days, I would attend the first annual Denver Pop Festival and get tear-gassed and beaten with a riot baton. I would also hear a lot of great music and see many strange sights.

I took my first acid trip at a place called The Cavern, or The Cave. It was brown Czechoslovakian acid and I really enjoyed it. I originally took it because the guy told me it would make me crazy. I had been in the clutches of reality for too long. It didn't work; I had fun, but no crazy.

I drove back to Utah in my 1960 VW camper van with a new engine that I put in myself the day I got out of the army. When I arrived at the house, I soon discovered I did not fit there anymore.

I got in touch with some old friends from North Summit High School, Jackie and Dee, and told them about Nam and how great pot was. They could not believe that I could do such a thing. And they bet me $100.00 that I couldn't find any of "that" in Utah. I took their bet.

The next night we drove to Sugar House Park in Salt Lake City. I drove up to a VW van with California plates and, in less than a minute, I had some of "that" plus $100.00. I then took them out into the middle of nowhere and smoked them out.

Within two weeks, my mother was bugging me about getting a job and a haircut. I left for San Diego within the week. My father had moved there and it had to be better than Utah. I moved to San Diego in 1970. I lived in my van in the driveway in Chula Vista, California

I got in contact with someone whose name I had been given in Vietnam by a Hispanic friend. Soon, I moved to the Otay Mesa area, right next to the border. I called the number and gave them a password so they knew I was okay. I was told to wait at a certain location and someone would contact me.

Soon a 1960s Impala—long low and cool—pulled up. A young Mexican introduced himself and said, "My uncle says you're okay." With that, he got out and opened the huge trunk and inside, under a blanket, were three rows of kilos, all wrapped in different colors of cellophane: red, blue and green.

"My uncle says the green ones are the best this week," he said. I chose three of the green ones. They were $60.00 per kilo, or over 2 lbs. each, and good weed. I got 36 five-finger lids out of each.

I stayed in San Diego till 1975, and got married to a Navy brat and rode motorcycles. Mine was a chopped 1969 Triumph 650. I grew my hair long and dressed like a biker.

I was working at Rohr Corporation in Chula Vista as an aircraft sheet-metal mechanic. I joined the union and worked on both sides of a strike. I got laid off on all of the holidays and rode my chopper in the wonderful weather.

I soon found a new job working on a tuna boat out of the San Diego harbor. We fished the Sea of Cortez and around the Bonita islands.

We would load some square fish (kilos) on the very bottom of the load, where they would be hidden from prying eyes until we took them out. Then we would catch 8 to 11 tons of fish and off-load at the fish depot, pass inspection and off we would go into the ether.

I used a lot of the skills I learned in the army to adjust to my new life.

I moved to Oregon and got a job in the local sawmill. Soon, my wife joined me for another try. We stayed together until 1977 and then we divorced.

I moved back to Utah with everything I owned in the back of a 1946 International flathead six-cylinder truck. It broke down on the Idaho-Utah border. I called my stepfather and he came and got me, but I had to leave the broken truck. I still miss that truck.

I was back in Utah again; I soon found a house to buy and a girl to marry. I bought a log cabin three miles outside of Henefer, Summit County, Utah.

I was now living where my father, grandfather, and great-grandfather had lived. I was related to everyone in Henefer, as well as most of Coalville and Morgan. Both my parents had lots of kids and cousins, aunt and uncles.

This can be very good if you need help, but when they are bored with their lives, they will fixate on yours—and watch your every move. They had a million questions that were none of their business.

I got a job at the Ideal Cement Company, thanks to my stepfather, who had worked there for 46 years. He vouched for me, but he made me promise I would not embarrass him. I don't think I did. I worked there for 11 years and still get a small retirement check from them.

CHAPTER 14
Comedy Years

The first time I told my new wife I was a Vietnam vet, she said, "I didn't know they had that many sick animals over there."

While I was working, I was also performing as a stand-up comic in Salt Lake City. It was quite a learning experience.

I used it instead of psychotherapy; the one thing you learn really fast is that audiences are brutally honest.

The first time I went onto the stage, I wore my field jacket, with my hat pulled down to cover my eyes. I really enjoyed the eight years I performed, but at a certain point, you must decide what you want and work toward it.

Some of the agents wanted me to move to LA, but I did not

want to be in show business anymore. I had a lovely wife and I chose that life.

But I was desperate to get out of Utah again, so I moved to a little town above Seattle, Washington, called Granite Falls.

I found out later that a lot of Vietnam veterans had moved there because of the trees and isolation. I did a little comedy but decided I did not need that anymore, and I began to seek help for my PTSD.

I had first tried to get help in the early 1980s, but in Salt Lake City, Utah, all they could or would do was get you into a discussion group. Just talk. I vowed that I would never go to them again. And I didn't, until I had a complete breakdown, both physical and mental.

I was working as a carpenter, and I had a seizure while descending a ladder. I fractured my right elbow. When I came out of the anesthetics, the surgeon told me I would never be able to use a hammer or any hand tools again with my right arm.

Well, there went my livelihood. I went into a long and deep depression. I was going to Canada and getting extra codeine so I could stay numb.

I finally went for help when my very wise wife asked me, "If you broke your arm, you would go to a doctor and have it fixed. Why not your head?"

I went to my counselor and asked for help and was admitted to 7-East in the Seattle VA Hospital. I was admitted and spent two weeks in the hospital and started taking one of many in a long line of antidepressants and began counseling on a weekly basis.

I went to two different counselors. One was from Blackfoot, Idaho, and after counseling me for over a year, he told me, "I will not support you 100% because everyone I've ever helped get 100% has destroyed their lives with drugs, and so will you." In my head, I screamed, "Fuck you," and I left his office and never saw him again.

Frank O Stephens

He called me and interrupted one of my wife's sessions with her counselor (they were in the same building) to tell me he "needed closure."

My wife told him, "You have been seeing my husband for over a year and if you think he is coming back to your office, you really don't know Frank."

Fuck his closure.

I went to his former partner, who didn't have a good thing to say about him; on that we agreed. Within six months, I had filed and received a 10% decision. It took me six years to get the 80% with unemployability that I have today.

CHAPTER 15
Sun Dance Years

SUN DANCE YEARS

While in Washington, I got involved with Native American ways.

I had been studying and reading books, and I found that the only groups of people who were successful at welcoming veterans back from war were the Native American tribes. I found out that when warriors returned to the village, they would send a runner to the village, and the people would gather and listen as the warriors told their stories and they shared the experience, both happy and sad.

I became a firekeeper for the for the Veterans Lodge in Maryville, Washington, on the Tulalip Indian Reservation. My friend Joseph and I kept that fire for seven years and we learned a lot of lessons.

My brother and friend, Tommy, asked me if I would go to the Sun Dance and support him. Of course I did, and thus began a 19-year quest that I am still on. I have completed a full four-year commitment and danced a few more years.

The Sun Dance is a Native American ceremony where the participants go without food and water for three days and nights. They dance in the sun and at any time, someone can "pierce."

In the practice of holding the skin and "piercing," they take a scalpel and cut a hole while pushing a buffalo-bone pin into your flesh.

You can pierce the chest above the nipples, the arms or the back.

I choose the chest and have two circles of scars. When the pins are in place, they tie your pins into a harness that you build and tie to a rope, which is suspended from the sacred Sun Dance tree.

Then you stand up and dance until you are ready to break, then you dance backwards until the pins tear out of your flesh.

It is a test of your concentration and intent. You must pull yourself off or try until you have nothing left. If you cannot break, two big guys will grab you and assist you to break.

I have danced in at least 19 dances and pierced in almost all of them and never needed help breaking.

In our way of belief, all you really have to give to the Creator is your flesh and suffering. The rest—money and words—are empty and easy.

I carried the veterans' staff for 15 years. I was asked to make it by Lakota Elders. The staff was beautiful and a very serious undertaking. I built a classic crook-shaped staff with otter fur wrapping and golden eagle feathers, donated by the veterans. Some were blood feathers; they are feathers that are used to count coup on a dead enemy (coup feathers). Also, there was a lot of red cloth for all the blood that has been spilled for this country. My task was to award feathers to warriors who had been in combat.

I have no feathers myself.

As a white (sort of) guy, I cannot possess these sacred feathers. The tribal leaders gave them to me to be awarded to the men.

At one dance, I awarded feathers to a man who had taken pictures of the atomic bomb that had caused his leg to be amputated. We wheeled him into the scared circle and awarded him a feather.

As I tied the feather in his wispy white hair, I whispered in his ear, "From a grateful family and grateful nation, we award you this feather. Thank you, and we love you." We all cried.

His wife told me she had been married for over 50 years and this was the first time she had seen him cry. He told me "This is the first time my country has ever thanked me." I also awarded feathers to his nephew who had been a helicopter pilot in Vietnam and to a young man who was heading to Afghanistan. This is a terrible continuum of violence and death.

I am very honored to be allowed to worship at these altars and be welcome in these communities. The Native Americans have put up a 500-year resistance to our thieving ways. They, as a group, have provided more great warriors for this nation than almost any group. They and the Black people are both warrior peoples. They have been exploited for their warrior spirit, and then cheated when it comes to Medals. That's America for ya. I intend to attend a dance next year in Southern California that is full of veterans and, which, I am told, holds them in great honor. I will go and see.

I appeared in a *New York Times* article, dated Thursday, August 26, 2004, by Timothy Egan, titled "Wounds Opened Anew as Vietnam Resurfaces."

> "It really upsets me, pitting one veteran against another," said Frank Stephens, 55, of Granite Falls, Wash., who received a Purple Heart after being wounded in Vietnam in 1969. "I feel like the politicians are using us. They won't let that war go."
>
> Mr. Stephens, a former army specialist from Granite Falls, who was wounded by shrapnel from a land mine, describes himself as an independent.
>
> He had never harbored any bitterness toward his fellow baby boomers who did not serve, but the Swift Boat controversy has made him rethink his feelings toward people like Vice President Dick Cheney, who avoided the draft by five college deferments.

"The vice president said he had 'other priorities,'" said Mr. Stephens, gesturing toward his war wound. "Didn't we all?"

"Rant!"

Now that we are here, I would like to vent some steam. The current president, Trump, is in the same category as Dick Cheney: he is a physical and moral coward. Willing to send young men to die, but not them or their families. Shame on you.

Another person I can't stand is Ted Nugent—fucking hypocrite, isn't he? He could have served but he was too cowardly and greedy to go and help fight. So, he takes his guilt and shame out on the animals he kills and then feeds his guilt posing with homeless veterans in his photo ops. Fuck him and his tainted meat.

Why doesn't he take some of his money and build a homeless shelter or give it to a homeless veteran?

CHAPTER 16
Family History

MOM AND DAD 1944

GRANDPA AND GRANDMOTHER STEPHENS,
AFTON 1940 temperature is -20* F.

Frank O Stephens

I sit here today with both ends of my father's life: I have his birth certificate and his death certificate, and it is hard for me to ignore the similarities in our paths.

I was born in Afton, Wyoming, Star Valley, Lincoln County—a small valley in the northwest part of Wyoming against the Idaho border. The Butch Cassidy Gang took advantage of this location. They lived with women on one side of the border and robbed the other side; the authorities could not pursue them across state lines.

My grandfather, Otto Thomas Stephens, was born in 1896 and lived until 1980. He had been a government trapper; had a swing band during prohibition; was a car mechanic for the movie business in Hollywood; owned Kimball Junction in Northern Utah; and started, named and managed Little America, at the time the world's largest gas station in the world.

He then moved to Afton and started, or bought and remodeled, The Otto Stephens Cowboy Club and The Golden Spur Cafe.

He imported Chinese cooks into Wyoming in 1950. He had learned about these cooks from his son-in-law, Ed Harris (RIP), who had been the OSS station chief in Singapore during and after WWII.

"Grand Opening For 'Golden Spur' Will Be Held Saturday," reads the headline in *The Star Valley Independent* for Saturday, May 20, 1950.

> "A grand opening is scheduled for Afton's new modern café, the "Golden Spur," recently completed by Mr. Otto Stephens. Although the café has been operating since last Sunday, the grand opening will nevertheless be an

event to formally introduce this fine eating place to the public.

250 orchids will be given away by the management to all ladies who eat there, starting at 1 p.m. until all are gone. The Golden Spur is being operated by Mr. Young S. Hong, and Charley Hong, professional Chinese cooks. Chinese and American dishes are featured at prices that are "in line," as can be evidenced by a sample menu elsewhere in this paper.

Mr. Stephens welcomes everyone to come in and see the place, and enjoy the fine food. Over 100 persons can be accommodated.

Grandfather hired Mr. Young S. Hong and his assistants, Henry Louie and Charley Hong. Professional Chinese cooks. They left their families and moved to Wyoming.

I remember being in the third or fourth grade and hurrying down to the Golden Spur and being taken into the back of the restaurant, where Charlie, would feed me the most amazing meals that tasted wonderful.

I was "Number One Grandson," and they treated me very well.

At first all of their yelling and gesturing with a meat cleaver in their hands was a little intimidating for a young cowboy.

I was already getting ready for Vietnam.

GRANDPA OTTO FISHING

My grandfather Otto was, to this day, the best fisherman I have had the privilege of watching do his ballet of motion and grace. "Kingfish," he would say, "watch the bugs on the river. See how they gently touch the water?" I watched and learned.

He took me to the water's edge and turned over rocks to patiently answer my questions. Then he would produce from his fishing vest the most perfect fly that looked exactly like the bugs touching the water.

It was never very long until he was fighting a big brown or rainbow trout into his woven creel, which I still treasure. I was lucky to end up with his fishing equipment; what a gift. I have fished and caught a lot of fine tasting trout with his equipment.

Kick Em In The Guts

I got my nickname from the Kingfish character on the *Amos 'n' Andy* radio show. I would go with Grandpa when he went on his "trapline," which was his string of coin-operated machines and jukeboxes that he had scattered from Rock Springs to Thermopolis, up over the Hoback pass. And of course, Jackson Hole.

I had the pleasure of being able to walk into any bar that Grandpa was in and they would seat me at the bar and serve me a nonalcoholic drink of my choice. The old cowboys of the 1940s and 1950s were some of my earliest friends; I wish my memory was better so I could remember all of the stories they told me. Grandpa gave a fish fry every year for the whole of Star Valley at the fish hatchery with the Department of Fish and Game helping him. Those were great times.

While I was growing up, my father, Vaughn Otto Stephens, was training Arabian horses for the rich people in Salt Lake City, Utah. There were always wonderful horses around and my father was one of the best riders I have ever seen. When he rode, he became part of the horse. It was graceful and smooth.

My father had been in the Pacific Theater in the Philippines in Leyte Gulf and other battles. He attained the rank of CWO (Chief Warrant Officer) in the US Army, in an artillery outfit. He was in the 96th Infantry Battalion, "The Dead Eyes." He was proud of what he had done, but he had a problem with his relationship with alcohol.

He had moved away from Utah because of their liquor control laws, and he couldn't get enough to drink so we moved.

Thinking back all those years ago, I had an ideal childhood: outdoors, hunting and fishing in the high country of the west. We moved back and forth between Salt Lake City Utah and Afton, Wyoming, until I was in eighth grade, in junior high school.

One morning, I awoke to hear my mom scream, "Oh no!" and begin sobbing. When I asked what was wrong, she handed me the paper. And there in *The Salt Lake Tribune* on Monday, January 28, 1963, was an article titled: "Alarm Traps Trio in S.L. Apartment." And there, for the world to see, was my father being led on a perp walk in handcuffs. He had been arrested by the SLC police.

My father, along with two of his drunk friends, had decided to rob the apartment of a rich man. I was humiliated and embarrassed.

"I can't go to school. What will my friends say?" I blurted out.

"If they are truly your friends, they will still be your friends," my mother said.

Wisdom for sure, but hard for a teenager to hear. Of course, she was right. I went to school, and it was a little rough, but I survived.

In the next few weeks, things really changed. My mom and dad divorced. My mom began to date, and she ended up marrying a former friend of my father's and a man who had proposed to her sister (my aunt turned him down).

Monroe (RIP) lived in Henefer, Utah, and had all of his life. My grandmother and grandfather on my mother's side also lived there. It was a return to her roots for my mom. I was not happy to move to a small town after living in a big city like Salt Lake City. But my mom helped me buy a car: a four-door '53 Chevy. Green-on-green paint with a six-cylinder and three on the tree. I felt like I had died and gone to heaven.

I was already on the swim team, diving from the 1m and 3m boards at South High in SLC. So, when I moved to Henefer, I was happy to learn that the high school in Coalville, about 11 miles east of Henefer, had just built a brand-new Olympic-sized swimming pool, with both a 1m and 3m board.

In high school, I lettered in football, wrestling, and swimming. I was kind of a jock. Just the kind of kid that the army wanted. When I think of the arc of my life, I was trained and programed for the service. Even the rifle I learned to shoot with was an H&K that weighed exactly the same as an M1, a little over 9 lbs. It had a 9-shot magazine and peep sights just like the real thing. My father had won it in the army for winning a shooting contest.

I spent a lot of my younger life in the woods and mountains around me. I watched deer and elk in Wyoming, and in Utah I saw black bears and grizzly bears in the wild, as well as moose with their giant antlers from another time and their forlorn look. I was lucky enough to know the game warden who fed the elk and buffalo herds in Alpine, Wyoming, and he allowed me to ride in the sleigh and feed them. It was a thrill for a young man to be surrounded by large mixed herds of buffalo and elk.

I could not have had a more ideal childhood if I had written it for myself, outside in the high-mountain air. Afton is in a wonderful valley that is 50 miles from Jackson Hole. The water supply for the town is Swift Creek, which is fed by one of only two cold water geysers in the entire world. The water is so cold when it gushes from the ground that you can hardly drink it.

My father and I never did much together until the end of his life, the last six months. I regret not spending more time with him, but I was a kid; I had no choice. My grandfather took me under his wing and let me hang around. I watched as he expertly tied the most delicate flies. He allowed me to free-form and tie any kind of flies I wanted. Oh, my goodness, they were big and flashy! I got the biggest hook I could find, and I tied the longest and most colorful feathers on with neon-colored thread. It would have taken a fish the size of a whale to take one of those flies, but all he said was, "Good job, Kingfish. All we have to do is find a fish big enough to eat it."

When we would go on his trapline, we would drive his '56 Chrysler New Yorker station wagon. It was like a tank, had a Hemi engine and could scare the hell out of a young kid. Grandpa drove like a madman. He would cross the center line, saying, "I was driving on these roads before they put lines on 'em."

My father went hunting every year and usually got a deer and an elk. As long as I can remember, I have been eating jerky.

We would have a quarter to a half of an elk made into jerky at K&B Cold Storage, where we had a locker. I recall the slightly metallic smell of the frozen meat, along with the smell of fresh wood chips on the floor.

I would sit and watch my dad read. He read everything he could, two books at a time, and he had total recall of every word, comma and period. Around his chair, there were vast stacks of books. A lot of Zane Grey and Louis L'Amour. He would invite me to pick up any book and turn to any page I chose, tell him what page and what line, and he could tell me the word or sentence that was there. He had an extraordinary mind, but he wasted it and drank himself to death without ever really using his talents. I inherited a lot of his talents. I am grateful for all the gifts from the past generations.

My father, Vaughn Otto Stephens, died at age 64. His obituary reads:

> Vaughn Otto Stephens, 64, of Afton, died Tuesday, Jan 3, 1984, at his home of a heart attack. Funeral services were held Friday, Jan. 6, at 10 a.m. in the Afton Second Ward with Bishop Paul Stauffer officiating. Burial was in Henefer, Utah. He was born April 19, 1919, in Henefer, Utah, to Otto and Beatrice Stephens. He attended schools in Coalville, Utah, where he graduated in 1939. He married Rhea Jaques in Feb. 1942, and they divorced in 1965. He married Leone Stoker in Sept. 1965. He was a member of the Church of Latter-day Saints. He trained and rode horses. He also enjoyed hunting and fishing. He worked as a salesman. He was a member of the Star Valley Fire Department. He served in the US Army, where he earned the rank of Warrant Officer. He received the Asiatic Pacific Campaign Medal with two bronze stars, the Philippine Liberation Ribbon with two bronze stars, American Defense Medal, American Campaign Medal, World War II Victory Medal and the Meritorious Service Unit Plaque. He is survived by his wife Leone of Afton; son Frank Otto Stephens of Henefer, Utah; mother Beatrice Stephens of Afton; and sister Mrs. Ed (Jean) Harris of Roy, Utah, and one grandchild.

CHAPTER 17
Return to Ambush Site

AMBUSH SITE 2019

WAR MEMORIAL AND NVA CEMETARY 2019

In Jan 2, 2019, I was preparing for my 15th trip back to Vietnam. My girlfriend and I were leaving Feb. 12, 2019, and would travel by van to some of the places I was in 1968, where I was in contact with the NVA. I expected to have some very profound experiences.

So much has changed, both in Vietnam and in my understanding of the war's relationship to me and the Vietnamese people.

Now they are not only my friends, but my loved and honored family. I looked forward to seeing my son, Trong, and his lovely wife, Le, and their sons, James and Ben, mother Thong, and father Mot. They truly make me feel welcome both in their country and in their hearts.

Most of my other trips had been solo or with my wife before she passes in 2011. This time we were traveling with another couple, Daryl and Michelle—friends from Washington State—and two Marine vets, who hadn't been back since their combat tours. George and Mikel Amiotte are cousins from South Dakota. They are Native American. I had met George maybe three or four times at the Sun Dance over the years.

George told Mike we were old Sun Dance friends who had known each other for 20-plus years. But that is George. His teachers were some of the most respected and traditional of the Lakota Elders. We were meeting up in Hoi An, Vietnam, one of my favorite places on earth.

"The Return Trip"

We arrived in Vietnam just after Tet, Feb. 13, 2019, and returned to San Francisco, April 2, 2019. We flew into Saigon, also known as Ho Chi Minh City. My girlfriend and I and Daryl and Michelle, checked into our hotel, The Liberty Central, run by the Odessa group, a Russian mafia group that invested its money in Vietnam. They run great hotels, very secure.

My son Trong met us and rented us a 12-passenger van for us and our luggage, plus a driver. It cost us about $1000.00 for the whole trip from Saigon to Hoi An.

The first day we just ate and toured around District 1, and went to Ben Thanh Market for some food and snacks. We left Saigon on Feb. 16, 2019, and drove to Ban Me Thuot. I had never been on this stretch of Hwy 14, so it didn't bring back any memories.

At the south end of Ban Me Thuot, things looked more like I remembered. We stayed in a very nice high-rise hotel with "Luxury" in the name. We were on the 11th floor and overlooked the whole town; I didn't know it, but I was overlooking the place where the ambush happened 50 years ago.

What gigantic changes have occurred. America, as a country, had basically flattened, or poisoned, most of the farmable land in Vietnam. But as I looked out across the Central Highlands of Vietnam in February 2019, I saw, from horizon to horizon, a garden consisting of hundreds of thousands of garden plots: a patchwork of fields carefully tended by women in conical hats. There are four main crops in the Central Highlands: coffee, rubber, pepper and cashew nuts. Vietnam is the world's second-largest exporter of coffee and also the second-biggest exporter of rice, just behind Thailand.

There were no other Westerners in the city, but Trong took good care of us. We hired a car and a guide to show us around. We drove through a lot of those well-tended gardens and took in some beautiful waterfalls.

We stopped for some coffee next to one of the gardens and took an impromptu tour of the garden, when, from above our heads, came the unmistakable "Fuck you" of the Taegu lizard. I was not crazy; they all heard it! I had told people about this lizard my whole life and now they were seeing it and hearing it.

I was astounded back in 1968 that these lizards yelled obscene words at you in English. That takes a certain kind of cunning to mess with your mind through a lizard. Making a weapon of a reptile.

We found the spot where I was ambushed and it has been turned into a cemetery for Vietnamese war dead—heroes who gave their lives to defend their country from me, an American invader.

I now understand why they fought so hard and long for their land where their ancestors' bones are buried.

The Vietnamese are, for the most part, casual about religion, but they all praise their ancestors on certain days and try to return to their ancestral homes for Tet. This is one reason the American war was so damaging to the Vietnamese army and people. When a B-52 drops a 500 or 1000-pound bomb, there is not much left of the human body if hit directly. How do you gather up vaporized people so that they can they be buried and then praised by their family later? Answer is, you can't—thus leaving a big blank in that family's story. And it leaves them with no place to praise that ancestor.

The Vietnamese lost about 3.5 million people in the American war, and more died because of the Agent Orange that was sprayed all over the country, as well as other chemicals left on and in the soil.

The Vietnamese people are still paying a high price for our fear of them.

On our trip to Vietnam in 2019 the American and Vietnamese were still cleaning up the Agent Orange–contaminated soil from the Da Nang airport, so the damage continues from 1968 to this day—over 50 years of damage.

We ended up driving to the Mewal Plantation, and although the rubber trees are gone, the land has been repurposed into a war memorial and cemetery for Vietnamese war dead, and the stream we crossed has been dammed off and is now a small lake that the neighborhood uses for fishing and irrigation.

This trip was about putting the war to rest for me. This has been a long and very rewarding journey throughout my life.

I have returned 15 times since my first trip in 2000, and the changes I have seen are very profound and far-reaching.

The Vietnamese are a fusion society: a mix of very ancient and cutting-edge, brand-new technology answering ancient needs.

As we traveled north on Hwy 14 toward Pleiku, the road looked more and more familiar, and my body tensed up in several places where I had been shot at in the past. My unit served as security for a lot of convoys between Pleiku and Ban Me Thuot in 1968.

Pleiku is not much of a tourist town and we didn't stop. There is almost nothing left from the time I was there; all the buildings were torn down and repurposed into new homes.

West toward the Cambodian border is the Oasis Fire Support Base where I was stationed for a good part of my tour.

It was there that I had my seizure, after which I was flown to Cam Ranh Bay, then Japan and eventually home.

But from the research I have done, there is nothing left to identify the base, so I said a silent prayer and drove on to Kon Tum.

We stayed in Kon Tum. It is a hill town, and we did not like the hotel and the vibe was much less friendly. We only stayed one night and then drove on to Da Nang, and then Hoi An.

In Hoi An, we stayed at three different hotels and then took a motorcycle trip over the Hai Van Pass to Hue and stayed there a few days. Then we went back to Hoi An for the rest of our stay until March 31, 2019, then it was on to Saigon and home on April 2, 2019.

While in Hoi An, we welcomed back three Marine veterans who had not been back since 1968. Two of the men, George and Mikel Amiotte, had told me they really needed to go back and put some closure on the war. The third I will not mention, as it was a waste of my time and his, as he did not "get it."

I will never take anyone with me to Vietnam again, other than my significant other, because it is like herding cats. Instead, I will meet them there and help them with their reservations and enjoy my time in the sun.

PHOTO TABLE OF CONTENTS

#1***Image1jpg: AUTHOR AND RAT ROD***
#2***Image2jpg: MIKE AND FRANK WITH HORSE***
#3***Image3jpg: FRANK ON PONY***
#4***Image4jpg: LITTLE COWBOY***
#5***Image5jpg: VAUGHN STEPHENS IN CLASS A UNIFORM***
#6***Image6jpg: FRANK STEPHENS IN CLASS A UNIFORM***
#7***Image7jpg: BASIC TRAINING GRADUATION***
#8***Image8jpg: FORT KNOX***
#9***Image9jpg: FRANK IN ROOM***
#10***Image10jpg: B40 IN***
#11***Image11jpg: B-40 OUT-DAMAGE INSIDE***
#12***Image12jpg: FRANK AND HIS MAU DUCE***
#13***Image13jpg: MIKE WITH AK-47***
#14***Image14jpg: FRANK WITH AK-47***
#15***Image15jpg: CAPTURED WEAPONS***
#16***Image16jpg: PRISONER***
#17***Image17jpg: RECOILESS RIFLE***
#18***Image18jpg: ME AND MY MONKEY***
#19***Image19jpg: VIETNAMESE LADIES CIRCA 1969***
#20***Image20jpg: FRANK AND ILENE 1968***
#21***Image21jpg: MUD IN BAN ME THOUT***
#22***Image22jpg: COX AND MISKA***
#23***Image23jpg: MISKA WITH MORTAR TUBE***
#24***Image24jpg: MORTAR TRACK HOME FOR 9 MONTHS***
#25***Image25jpg: JIM BRYANT PLACING A CLAYMORE MINE***
#26***Image26jpg: TED COLFER***

#27***Image27jpg: SIR OUR FAVORITE LT.***
#28***Image28jpg: BOXIE***
#29***Image29jpg: PLATOON SARGENT ROY YOUNG***
#30***Image30jpg: RON MISKA***
#31***Image31jpg: JEFF, DARELL, COLFER***
#32***Image32jpg: THE BLONDE TANKER-JERRY COLE***
#33***Image33jpg: BOXIE AND MISKA***
#34***Image34jpg: PORK A.K.A. GARY RUDDER, DARELL COLE***
#35***Image35jpg: LT. PLUMBER & DOC***
#36***Image36jpg: FRANK, GARY RUDDER AND UNKOWN***
#37***Image37jpg: ATTITUDE CHECK***
#38***Image38jpg: TRIBAL SOLIDIER***
#39***Image39jpg: TRIBAL BURIAL***
#40***Image40jpg: B TROOP ACENDS HILL-TRACK***
#41***Image41jpg: B TROOP ACENDS HILL-TANK***
#42***Image42jpg: ME ACTING COOL***
#43***Image43jpg: SE SONG RIVER KON TUM VIETNAM***
#44***Image44jpg: MIKE HAGER***
#45***Image45jpg: CHRISTMAS 1968 LZ OASIS***
#46***Image46jpg: DUST OFF***
#47***Image47jpg: CHIEU HOI PASS-FRONT***
#48***Image48jpg: CHIEU HOU PASS-BACK***
#49***Image49jpg: VILLAGE CHILD APRIL,2000***
#50***Image50jpg: TRONG AND FAMILY***
#51***Image51jpg: SUNDANCE YEARS***
#52***Image52jpg: MON AND DAD 1944***
#53***Image53jpg: GRANDPA AND GRANDMA STEPHENS 1940 AFTON WY. TEMP IS -20*F.***
#54***Image54jpg: GRANDPA OTTO STEPHENS FISHING***
#55***Image55jpg: AMBUSH SITE 2019***
#56***Image56jpg: WAR MEMORIAL & NVA CEMETARY 2019***

CPSIA information can be obtained
at www.ICGtesting.com
Printed in the USA
LVHW071810180723
752689LV00010B/134